NICOLA PITTAM is a British screenwriter, an award-winning author and a former Fleet Street journalist. Her TV pilot *House of the Rising Sun* (inspired by the lyrics of The Animals' hit song) made the Bitch List 2019 and was also placed on the inaugural Grey List 2023 of Hollywood's top 40 writers over 40. It was also placed in the semi-finals of both the Shore Scripts TV contest and the Los Angeles International Screenplay Awards.

Also by Nicola Pittam

Vow of Silence (with Suzanne Walsh)
George and Me (with Angie Best)
Christian Bale (with Harrison Cheung)

THE REBEL PIANIST OF MAJDANEK

A Holocaust Story of Music and Survival
in a Nazi Death Camp

Nicola Pittam

Published in 2024 by Mardle Books
15 Church Road
London, SW13 9HE
www.mardlebooks.com

Text © 2024 Nicola Pittam

Paperback ISBN 9781802471915
eBook ISBN 9781802472080

A CIP catalogue record for this book is available from the British Library.

Every reasonable effort has been made to trace copyright-holders of material reproduced in this book, but if any have been inadvertently overlooked the publishers would be glad to hear from them.

Printed in the UK

10 9 8 7 6 5 4 3 2 1

MIX
Paper | Supporting responsible forestry
FSC
www.fsc.org
FSC® C171272

This book is dedicated to Mosha and the six million Jews who were murdered during the Holocaust.

INTRODUCTION

I first came across Mosha's story on a blog while I was researching another true-life project. I'm generally not a very emotional person; I have that classic British stiff upper lip, which usually serves me well as a news journalist who has covered such tragedies as the Columbine school shooting and 9/11.

Yet, as I read Mosha's story, I just broke down crying. I don't know why it affected me the way it did, but I knew I just had to find out more about it. So the journalist in me went into overdrive, and within an hour I'd found that the story was from a book called *The Beethoven Factor* by Dr Paul Pearsall. I immediately ordered the book on Amazon and waited impatiently for it to arrive.

But after it arrived, I was surprised that Mosha was just one of a dozen or so case studies in Dr Pearsall's book, which is a psychological study of 'hardiness, happiness, healing and hope'.

Basically, Dr Pearsall was a licensed clinical neuropsychologist (and bestselling *NY Times* author many times over) who realised after counselling patients who had survived the Holocaust and cancer that many of them had stories to tell about how they had thrived in the face of adversity. For Mosha, that was thanks to music. Or, more specifically, the music of Beethoven.

Mosha's story was just a two-page case study in the book, but it affected me profoundly and I wanted to know more, not only about her but also about the Holocaust. But first I reached out to Dr Pearsall's estate, and they very kindly granted me the film rights to Mosha's story.

From there, Mosha's story quickly took on a life of its own. Because there was so little personal information about Mosha in the book, I couldn't find any records of her, but that didn't stop me doing extensive research on concentration camps and how music played such a huge role in the lives of the Jewish inmates as they struggled every day to stay alive.

While Mosha was a piano prodigy who really was tortured by the Nazis for refusing to play her music for them, this is a fictionalised account of her time in the concentration camp. In my research, I've come across hundreds, if not thousands, of Jewish prisoners' stories, and every one of them is heartbreaking and very real.

I originally envisioned Mosha's story being a movie and began working on a screenplay. I completed the screenplay and it placed well in several competitions, but I felt there was so much more that wasn't being told in the script. You only have about 120 pages to get your vision onto the screen, so I went back to Dr Pearsall's estate, and they agreed to also grant me the rights to turn Mosha's story into a novel.

Now, hopefully, I've given not only Mosha a voice but also all the other prisoners who were murdered during this atrocity. I wanted to highlight Mosha's courage and bravery as she refused again and again to play for the Nazis. Even when they smashed her fingers, she still refused. While Mosha's story is unique because of the music, she was not alone in being beaten or executed for standing up to the

Nazis. These brave men and women, who were persecuted simply because of their faith, deserve to be heard.

Everyone should be aware of the horrific atrocities carried out against the Jewish community by the Nazis, and I hope that by reading Mosha's story – and learning about all the other six million victims murdered in the Holocaust, as well as the survivors – people will remember and never let history repeat itself.

1

Berlin, 1928

The majestic Konzerthaus rises up from the square. It strains towards heaven. An angel perches on the roof, ready to take flight in a chariot drawn by winged gargoyles, who stare down at the procession of Mercedes cars as they idle in front of Germany's most famous concert hall. French and German domed cathedrals on either side are a stark reminder that this is sacred ground. A statue of poet, philosopher and historian Friedrich Schiller keeps a watchful eye on arriving concertgoers. A few latecomers rush past the monument with no time to admire the allegories of History, Poetry, Philosophy and Tragedy keeping Schiller company. They sweep past Grecian columns, up the steps of a treasure of German neoclassical architecture and into the concert hall. The lobby is almost empty. A grandiose staircase sweeps up to the main hall. It's an interior of incredible opulence. Chandeliers, marble, gilded plasterwork and pastel-hued paintings all compete for attention.

But the concertgoers are not here to admire the hall. The last few people hurriedly take their seats. Lights dim. Darkness. A buzz of anticipation fills the air.

A spotlight dances over the audience – a brief glimpse of Berlin's elite society mixed with important military figures.

The hum of restlessness and boredom swirls around the hall as the all–male Berliner Philharmoniker stride to their places. A reflective glow illuminates the stage as the conductor proudly mounts his podium.

Silence finally falls across the audience behind him. He taps his wooden baton. A quick burst of polite applause. He raises his arms. Sweeps them downwards as Beethoven's Ninth Symphony fills the hall. Tiaras and medals twinkle in time with the composer's most famous movement, 'Ode to Joy'. The chorale chimes in. Their blended notes dance around the room, bounce off the mahogany rafters. Seats inlaid with gold vibrate as the music crescendoes.

The spotlight suddenly illuminates Mosha Gebert, seventeen.

Her long, dark hair and pale skin reflect the ebony and ivory keys of the Steinway grand piano in front of her. She fidgets in her dusky-pink evening gown. It cost more than most families make in a month, yet hangs awkwardly on her lithe frame.

Nervous, she clenches then flexes her fingers several times. She looks out over the audience.

She's desperate to find a friendly face in the crowd. But all the faces blur into one. She knows she's on her own. She closes her eyes. Shuts out everything but the music.

Timidly, she begins her solo. Quiet and soft. Suddenly she transforms. Eyes fly open. Fingers dance across the keys. A masterful puppet of the melody. The orchestra slowly joins in. But this is Mosha's triumphant moment. This tiny waif of a girl is the leader now. Pent-up passion bursts out of her fingers. They fly across the keyboard with lightning speed. The tempo becomes more frantic, more urgent as Mosha becomes one with the music.

Josef Hanke, twenty-seven, already a *Hauptsturmführer* (Captain) in the Reichswehr army, sits in the front row just a few feet from Mosha. An immaculate uniform gives him an air of authority. A look of obsession transforms his face from steely to soft. Somehow, his intensity reaches Mosha. Their eyes lock. Mosha almost stumbles over the notes. But she refuses to let anything distract her focus. She breaks the gaze. The only thing that matters in this moment is the music. Cross with herself, Mosha pushes down even harder on the keys. Her anger only adds to the intensity.

Satisfied, Josef closes his eyes. He's instantly transported back in time to a mansion near Baden-Baden, twenty years earlier:

A stately home nestled in the mountains on the edge of the Black Forest. Turrets poke through the deep green foliage as Mosha's music continues to penetrate Josef's mind. A regal family crest billows from the highest tower as the wind whips through the trees.

Inside a room in the tower that would not look out of place in Berlin's Charlottenburg Palace, famous paintings adorn the walls. Every important German artist hangs here – Kollwitz, Liebermann, Friedrich. But child Josef, seven, ignores them all. He sits cross-legged on the floor. His sweet, cherubic face transfixed once more. He doesn't care that any one of these paintings would fund his privileged lifestyle for the rest of his life. His focus is on the middle of the room and a grand piano. A woman's elegant hands dance across the keyboard (in time with Mosha's music). Blush-pink nail polish gives the impression of daintiness. Yet there is great power behind the feminine appearance. Even the huge diamond ring on the wedding finger doesn't weigh down the speed and accuracy of her playing.

This is Josef's very glamorous mother, Greta, twenty-seven. She still has the looks that sparked proposals from princes and dukes during her debutante season ten years previously. But it's not her looks or her expensive soft pink silk gown that capture Josef's attention. It's the anticipation of what is to come.

Josef listens intently. Greta turns, beckons with her head. He hesitates. Greta stops. Holds out her arms and smiles encouragingly. He shuffles forward. She lifts him onto her lap. He squirms as she puts her arms around him. Gives him a little squeeze. Starts to play again.

Comfortable, Josef peacefully leans back into his mother's soft, warm body. He scrunches his eyes shut. Enjoys the intimacy. Presses against her as the tempo quickens.

As Mosha's music becomes more frenzied, Josef blinks. He's pulled out of the memory as the music comes to a climactic end. A female hand reaches across and rests on top of Josef's hands. Josef's eyes snap open. He looks warily to his left. His wife, Alice, twenty-five, sits next to him. Typically Aryan. Blonde hair, blue eyes. In any other era she'd be pretty. But she looks utterly dreary thanks to her clothes, the civilian version of military – grey, drab, lacklustre.

Her eyes are fixed straight ahead. Josef squeezes her hand. She doesn't squeeze back. He furtively checks the rest of the crowd around him. Quickly adjusts the cap perched in his lap. Alice's eyes quickly flick downwards, then back up to the stage.

Exhausted, Mosha slumps in her seat for a second. Then straightens, proud as a peacock. She turns to the audience. Desperate for adulation. Her eyes sweep over the crowd, careful to avoid Josef's piercing, hope-filled gaze.

First to his feet, Josef claps wildly. The rest of the audience quickly follows. Alice reluctantly stands and claps politely. Mosha shows no emotion as the applause washes over her. A quick bow, first to the crowd, then the conductor, before she hurries off stage. She allows herself a knowing smile at the deafening applause behind her.

2

Moments later, Mosha is ensconced backstage in the private, secure dressing room. Dozens of bouquets threaten to engulf the small room as Mosha sits in the middle of the flowers, ready to blossom into womanhood. She tries to ignore her boisterous younger sister, Celina.

Despite the age difference, Celina at thirteen is already more womanly than Mosha will ever be. Yet Celina jumps around with the exuberance of a child. Almost knocks over several of the vases. Mosha glares at their mother, Eva, thirty-six, a picture of poised elegance in a matching cerise gown – far too girlish in style for a woman her age. Eva raises a steely eyebrow. Celina immediately freezes. Slowly turns to Mosha. Celina exclaims, 'Did you see all of those people clapping for you?'

Mosha offhandedly replies, 'I saw them.'

Celina reaches out, grabs Mosha in a bear-like hug. Mosha stiffens. She hates physical contact of any kind. After a second, she gingerly hugs her sister back. Celina reluctantly lets go as Mosha pulls away. She rubs her hands, over and over again until they look red and raw. Eva instructs Celina, 'Get your sister her cream.'

Celina snatches a pot of expensive hand cream that's easily within Mosha's reach. A sacrificial offering, she holds out the pot with both hands. Mosha gently rubs it into her delicate hands as Eva asks, 'Do you want a drink?'

Mosha shrugs as Celina discards the pot and dashes over to a table laden with champagne and delicacies. She expertly pours a drink. Hands it to her sister. Celina turns to Eva. 'Can I have one?'

Celina grabs for a glass as Eva, in her sternest voice tells her, 'You're too young.'

But a pouting Celina insists, 'Just a sip.'

Mosha grins at her sister. 'Oh, let her have some!'

But Eva dashes Celina's grown-up hopes as she replies, scathingly, 'When she's earned it.' Celina throws herself into a chair; she's now a sullen adolescent.

A knock on the door turns all their heads. Eva nods at Celina. She flings open the door to reveal a harried stage manager waiting on the other side. The stage manager looks at the floor, the wall beyond, Eva, anywhere but at Mosha. He blurts out, 'Miss Gebert, there are several people waiting to meet you at the stage door, including that SS officer again. He's very insistent.'

Mosha looks cautiously over at Eva, who shakes her head. Sounding a little unsure, Mosha says, 'Um, I don't want to meet anyone.'

The stage manager opens his mouth to insist, but Eva quickly cuts him off. She snaps, 'Look at her! She's exhausted. She needs her rest.' Eva fixes the stage manager with a glacial stare until he scurries out of the room.

Mosha sinks back into a chair. She sighs as though she has all the weight of the world on her young shoulders. 'I am so sick of these people thinking they have a right to me,' she muses aloud.

Eva is quick to reassure her shining star. 'It's just because you're so wonderful, darling.'

But Mosha already has other things on her mind. 'Will we be home soon?'

'Just two more dates,' says Eva. Mosha pulls a rose out of one of the bouquets and twirls it around in her hand.

'Can we go to the summer house in Gdańsk?'

Eva smiles. 'Wherever you want.' Eva then takes Mosha's precious hands in hers and squeezes them tight. Ignores Mosha's wince.

Outside the concert hall, several well-dressed men linger; cigarette smoke engulfs them as they stand around, making idle chit-chat. The stage manager cracks open the door a few inches. They surge forward as one, all eager for a glimpse of Mosha.

Josef, a small box tightly in his grasp, pushes his way to the front. A few men give him sidelong glances, but no one dares challenge 'the Captain'. Except the stage manager, who blocks him as he announces, 'Miss Gebert will not be receiving guests this evening.'

A clearly furious Josef says, 'Let me in. I demand to see her.'

But the stage manager refuses to give him an inch. 'She doesn't want to see anyone.' There's a collective sigh of disappointment.

A few men grumble under their breath as they turn away, but Josef stands his ground. 'Did you give her my message?' The stage manager nods wearily. But Josef won't give up. 'There's no way she would refuse to see me.'

The stage manager takes a step back as he delivers the crushing news. 'But she did.'

Josef is stunned. He can't believe he has been turned down. The stage manager gives Josef a little shove backwards, then slams the door and leaves him out in the cold, shutting him off from the promise of sweet music. Furious, Josef throws the gift to the ground and stomps off towards his waiting car – and his wife, who is inwardly fuming.

3

Warsaw, Spring 1943
A sparse room; a hint of better days sits in the empty picture frames adorning the walls. Mosha, now thirty-one, stands in the corner next to an ancient piano – battered but the

most expensive item she owns. Her lithe, once boyish frame, now bony and angular, appears as worn down as her surroundings. Yet her once renowned beauty matches the spirit buried deep inside. Still there, struggling to hang on.

She glances out of the window at the once beautiful city, now in ruins. On one side of the street, many of the homes are empty, crumbling into disrepair. People stumble down the street. Once proud people, they now look like beggars: poorly dressed and malnourished.

An old woman, a raggedy blanket wrapped around her instead of a warm coat, drags herself along, shivering with cold. A child shuffles along with his exhausted mother. He cries from hunger, but she has nothing to stop the tears. Heavy footsteps behind them signal the cause of all this needless pain and misery. She yanks the boy to the side just in time as German soldiers march past, efficient and purposeful.

A Mercedes-Benz W31 car, Nazi Party swastika flags flying on the bonnet, cruises down the street as Mosha turns away from the window. She glances at her sister Celina, now twenty-nine, who sits in a corner, half the woman she used to be. Literally. Celina has lost her womanly curves, the only compensation she had to redeem her lack of musical talent.

There's a timid knock on the door. A young girl, Anna Scheiner, fourteen, slowly pushes the heavy door open. It creaks as she steps into the room. Anna, her innocence and naivety now the one bright spot in the room, smiles shyly at Mosha, who smiles back. The smile transforms Mosha's bleak features, a hint of the once proud piano virtuosa briefly flashes across her face. Mosha gestures towards the piano. Anna scurries across the room, drops her bag and takes a seat on the stool. Without any words, Anna begins softly to play Chopin's *Marche funèbre* (funeral march). Mosha stops her. 'Let's play something a little less funereal.'

Mosha picks up a tattered sheet of music. She turns to Celina. 'The patrol has gone past.'

Celina can barely muster the strength to argue, but she does anyway. 'I'm sick to death of potatoes.'

Mosha has had this argument a million times before and her answer is always the same. 'It's potatoes or nothing.'

Mosha crosses to a table, opens her purse and hands Celina some crumpled notes. Celina stares at the money in her hand. 'Just three złotys? And why do I always have to go?'

Mosha patiently explains, yet again. 'I have a lesson. And that's all we have left.' Celina snatches the money and mumbles as she heads out of the door. 'You always have lessons, so why don't we have more money?'

Mosha turns, smiles at Anna. Anna shyly looks down at the piano keys, takes a deep breath and says, 'Is it true you once played for the prime minister?'

Mosha smiles at the memory. 'Yes, I played for Józef Piłsudski. I played for many important people. I was the darling of Europe.'

Gaining confidence, Anna adds, 'When?'

Mosha looks wistfully out of the window before answering. 'A long time ago. A different time.'

Mosha places the sheet of music on the piano lid. A rare ray of sunshine through the window illuminates the title, 'Ode to Joy'. Sporadic bursts of gunfire echo in the distance. Anna looks at the sheet music. 'Do I have to play Beethoven?'

Mosha nods. 'Yes. He was the greatest and most influential composer ever to have lived.'

Anna exclaims instantly, 'But he was German!'

'He was,' says Mosha.

'So why do I have to learn him?' asks Anna, clearly confused.

'You will come to love him as I do,' says Mosha.

Anna screws up her nose in disgust. 'I don't want to play this,' she says.

Mosha presses on. 'Did you know he wrote most of his music when he was deaf?' Anna just looks at her. Mosha continues. 'He even conducted when he was deaf.'

Anna finally gives in and shows some interest. 'How?'

Mosha knows she now has Anna hooked and launches into the real lesson. 'It was towards the end of his life. He was gravely ill and totally deaf. He had the chance to conduct 'Ode to Joy'. Eyes closed, he kept conducting the orchestra even after the piece was finished and the audience were on their feet, clapping and cheering. Because he was deaf, he had no idea the audience were giving him a standing ovation. A singer from the choir had to step forward and turn him around so he could *see* the shouts of "Bravo!" At that moment, he saw how his music touched people. It transcended his sadness and brought joy to them. Do you see now?'

Anna looks a little confused. 'I guess.' But she has more interesting things on her mind. 'Will we ever play together on stage?'

Mosha laughs and says, 'When you've practised some more!' Mosha taps the piano. Anna plays the first few bars, the music still haunting even when played by a novice. A serene look comes over Mosha's face.

Suddenly, clattering footsteps on the stairs drown out the music. Three SS soldiers, all so baby-faced they wouldn't look out of place in the Hitler Youth, burst through the door. Mosha instinctively puts herself in front of Anna.

One of the soldiers strides forward, grabs Mosha by the arm. Starts to drag her away. She breaks free, rushes back to Anna, protectively puts her arms around her. The other soldiers step forward, try to prise the pair apart. Anna screams, 'No! No!'

One of the soldiers yells, 'Shut her up!' as Mosha cries out, 'Leave her alone.'

An SS general, old enough to know better but still young enough to be dazzled by a regime, appears in the doorway. The soldiers all stand to attention as Mosha and Anna huddle together as the general strides around the room, a predator circling its prey. He marches back and forth, toying with them. With every step, their terror increases. Mosha shields Anna's eyes as she turns the young girl's head into her bony chest.

As the general passes the pair for a fourth time, he grabs Mosha's hand, twists it until she cries out in pain. Then he shoves her so hard, she crumples to the floor. He grabs her arm, drags her to the other side of the room. Anna tries to cling to Mosha, but a soldier grapples with her, pins her arms behind her back. Anna sobs as she desperately tries to break free. But she's no match for these soldiers.

The general pulls Mosha to her feet by her hair. The pain on her face is unmistakable, but she refuses to cry out. Instead, she stares at him. This infuriates him. 'How dare you look me in the eye, you Jewish whore!' He strikes her hard across the face with the back of his hand.

The general nods to the soldier holding Anna, who manhandles her to the middle of the room.

The teen is terrified, not only of what is to come but of fighting back. Tears streak down Anna's face as she locks eyes with Mosha, who wrenches herself out of the general's grasp, flies across the room. But the general is just as quick. Before Mosha can grab Anna, he's by her side. His fist strikes her in the pit of her stomach, causing her to double over. She staggers, drops to her knees.

The general grabs Mosha's chin in his hand. Raises her head up, twists it so she looks directly at Anna. The soldier keeps a grip on Anna but holds her at arm's length. The general pulls a gun from his holster, points it at Anna. Mosha grabs for the gun, but the general swats her away like an annoying fly.

He laughs in her face as he points the gun back and forth between the two women. It's a game, but there can be no winner. The gun stops on Anna. Mosha screams, dives in front of Anna.

The general wryly says, 'How touching.' All the soldiers begin laughing.

Anna finds her courage, steps around Mosha. Defiant, she squares up to the general. 'I am not afraid.'

The general calls her bluff as he points his pistol and pretends to pull the trigger. Both Anna and Mosha scream. The general's laughter mingles with their cries as he strikes Anna with the pistol. She slumps to the floor. Blood gushes from a cut on her head. Mosha retches as she desperately tries to stop herself from being sick at the sight of Anna's blood.

The general looks distastefully at Mosha, then Anna, who has curled up in a foetal position on the floor. He raises the gun once more; this time he pulls the trigger for real.

Raising his voice above Mosha's screams, the general barks an order. 'Get her out of here.'

The soldiers rush forward, grab Anna's lifeless body, drag her out of the door, leaving a streak of blood behind.

Mosha's sudden anger is as red as Anna's blood. She flies across the room and beats the general on the chest with her fists, but he grabs her easily, holds her away from him. Mosha spits at him.

He strikes her across the face. Mosha sobs. 'She was just a girl.'

The general sneers. 'A Jewish girl.'

She looks him in the eye defiantly. 'I'm Jewish.'

The general snorts. 'And that is your misfortune. It will be your undoing too.' He pushes Mosha in front of him.

Mosha stumbles as he shoves her out of the front door of the building. Celina appears just as her sister is bundled into a waiting car. She sees Mosha, drops the potatoes, sprints towards her, crying out, 'Mosha! Mosha!' But the car door slams shut before Celina can reach it. Mosha stares from the back window as the car pulls away.

People try not to look as Celina drops to her knees, crying, as her whole world disappears around the corner. Suddenly, soldiers grab Celina from behind as a truck pulls up alongside them. One of them opens the back of the truck, pushes Celina inside, where several Polish Jews already huddle together. As the truck pulls away, Celina's eyes stay on Anna's limp body as it lies, alone, discarded in the gutter.

4

The fading dusk light casts an eerie glow over the train depot. A cloak of gloom and desperation hovers over hundreds of Jews – old, young, families – as they stand in line. As they shuffle forward as one, fear wraps itself tighter and tighter around them. Downtrodden. Starving. They clutch what few precious possessions they have left.

Mosha is marched to the front of the line. The general pushes her in behind the person at the head of the line. She's numb, but not from the cold. She has nothing but the clothes on her back. No family by her side, no possessions in her hands. She takes a step forward towards a makeshift table. A clerk sits at the table, writes in a ledger. Just beyond, a train patiently waits.

Mosha taps the shoulder of an old man, the only person in front of her. He turns. 'Where are they taking us?' she asks.

The old man looks at her as though she's crazy. He sighs. 'To our death. You've heard the stories. You know what happens.'

Of course Mosha's heard the stories but she still doesn't want to believe. 'The stories can't all be true,' she replies.

The old man shakes his head, approaches the table. After a brief exchange with the clerk, he walks towards the train, defeat clearly visible in the stoop of his shoulders. He stops. Turns to Mosha. Smiles sadly, tips his hat to her. *'B'ezrat HaShem.'*

Mosha approaches the table as a scuffle breaks out behind her. Two men are fighting over a dirty, threadbare coat. Soldiers quickly step in to break it up as Mosha stands in front of the clerk, who doesn't even bother to look up. 'Name?' Mosha hesitates. She looks around. 'Name!'

Mosha is confused. 'Don't you know who I am?'

Impatiently, the clerk says, 'No.'

Indignant, Mosha asks, 'Then why was I snatched out of my house? And shoved to the front of this line?'

The clerk finally looks up at her. 'I don't know. And I don't care. Now, what is your name?'

'I am Mosha Gebert,' she tells him.

The clerk holds out his hands. 'Papers?'

Mosha shrugs. 'I don't have them.'

The clerk tuts. 'Why not?'

Mosha tries to explain. 'I didn't have time—' as the clerk cuts her off.

'Occupation?'

Mosha looks at him, astounded. 'I was… I am a pianist.' The clerk is getting bored now; there are hundreds of people in line behind Mosha and most of them are getting as impatient as the clerk.

'When did you last play?'

Mosha admits, 'It's been a while—'

'So, what do you do now?'

Mosha insists, 'I'm a pianist.'

The clerk, clearly getting more annoyed by the minute, says, 'Where have you been working then?'

Mosha says, 'I've been teaching piano.'

The clerk writes in the ledger: *Mosha Gebert – TEACHER*. 'Second carriage.'

Mosha is confused. 'Second carriage?'

Without looking up, the clerk points to the train sitting down the track. 'Where are we going?' Mosha asks.

The clerk looks up at her, but ignores the question. He gestures to an SS soldier nearby, then nods at Mosha. 'Second carriage,' he says again. The soldier grabs Mosha, marches her over to the second carriage. Pushes her towards an open door. Helping hands reach out, help pull Mosha into the carriage. Inside, each third–class carriage is packed with more than a hundred Polish Jews, crammed like cattle into the tiny space. There are no seats, so people sit on the floor or stand to peer through tiny gaps in the wooden slats of the walls. The meagre covering of straw on the floor is already filthy.

Another two climb in after Mosha. The door bangs shut. If it was stuffy before, now it's unbearable in the cramped space, with no room to move. People hold on to their prized possessions – fur coats, expensive watches, precious packages of food – as they eye each other with distrust. It's not just the thin and starving packed in. Wealthy Jews are also squashed up against each other. Mosha struggles, but manages to squeeze herself into a corner, sits down next to a young woman, Zofia Ladowska, twenty, who clutches to her chest a stack of letters.

Zofia, too naïve for her own good, shyly smiles. She shows the letters to Mosha. 'They're letters from my husband. Every week he writes me a letter or poem.'

Her interest piqued, Mosha asks, 'Where is he now?'

Zofia chokes back tears. 'I don't know. They took him away while we were waiting for the train.'

For a moment, Mosha hesitates, unsure what to say. 'What's his name?' seems the best option.

Zofia sniffles. 'Jakub. He's a librarian.'

Mosha tries to reassure her. 'Then he'll be fine.'

But Zofia is adamant. 'No, you're wrong. They have no respect for books or for art. They have no respect for anything.' A tear slips down Zofia's cheek.

Mosha looks uncomfortable until Zofia asks her, 'What's your name?'

'Mosha.'

'I'm Zofia!'

Zofia dries her tears, pulls something from her pocket. She unwraps a handkerchief to reveal bread and cheese. Zofia is offering not just food but also friendship as she urges Mosha to take it.

So hungry, Mosha hardly chews as she gobbles it down. Zofia laughs. 'Slow down. Anyone would think you hadn't eaten in days.'

Mosha admits, 'I haven't.'

'You didn't get a chance to collect anything?' Zofia asks, adding, before Mosha can reply, 'I took everything I could. Not that we had much. We'd sold everything we had to buy food. But I still have this.'

Zofia opens the top of her dress; a necklace sparkles. Mosha leans forward, closes the dress. 'Don't show anyone else that.'

'Why not?' asks Zofia.

'I saw two men fighting over a dirty old coat, so I can only imagine what they would do to get their hands on that,' says Mosha.

Zofia nods. 'It'll get better when we get to the camp, right?'

Mosha doesn't know, but she can't admit that to a stranger. Instead, she changes the subject and asks, 'What happened to your family?'

'My parents only lived a few doors down, but when they pulled us out of our home and onto the street, I couldn't see them. What about your family?'

'My parents were taken months ago. But I'm sure we'll find our families once we get to the camp,' says Mosha.

Zofia smiles. 'Yes, we will.' Comforted, Zofia settles back, drifts off to sleep. But Mosha can't sleep. The horrors that await them keep her awake.

5

Nearly six hours later as the pre-dawn sun struggles to rise, the train slowly grinds to a halt as it pulls into a depot in the city of Lublin. Hundreds of identical-looking SS soldiers, all dressed in the same black uniform and all armed, stand to attention. A whistle blows and the soldiers effortlessly break into groups of twenty. Each group approaches one of the twenty carriages that are now sitting on the track.

The carriages open; people scramble out as quick as they can. Mosha and Zofia step down together onto the ground, slowly straighten up, stiff after hours sitting on the floor.

Mosha spies a sign attached to a low brick building but struggles to see what it says in all the turmoil as thousands of people swarm the platform. The soldiers start rounding people up into groups. Mosha and Zofia are slowly herded with the rest of their carriage along the platform and out of the sad and desolate building that passes for a train station.

Before they exit the station, Mosha turns back to look at the train and sees dozens of bodies being pulled from the carriages and just dumped on the side of the platform. She turns away but the image is seared in her brain. The soldiers begin pushing the prisoners into two lines but it's chaos as no one has any idea where they are going.

Suddenly, an SS general with a bullhorn appears. He yells, 'Get into line. Everyone get into line.'

People scramble to stand one behind the other. A few confused people wander away and ignore all orders to join the line. The general warns them twice. One or two older prisoners hear the second warning and dart back to the line. But several men have reached the edge of the road.

They don't look back as they take off across the field, foolishly hoping the longer grass will conceal them. But they don't get very far. Gunshots ring out. They drop to the ground. People start screaming. Pushing each other to get as far away from the soldiers as they can.

The general screams, 'STILL! Stand still or you will be shot too!' He fires his gun into the air.

The rabble calms down almost instantly. Scared families hug each other tight as parents try to hush their crying children and shield their eyes from the soldiers.

Now content they are in a more orderly line, the general gestures to the soldiers at the front. They begin walking. The general barks more orders: 'Follow the soldiers.' Everyone begins the trek to the camp.

It's only two kilometres away but it feels like forever. Most of the prisoners are already weak from malnutrition and are also tired from the train journey. Some stumble as they try to keep up with the march. Some are dragged along by their frightened family members. Mothers carry their crying children as best they can. When the load becomes too heavy, someone else takes over and helps make sure there's no need for any more gunfire.

After nearly an hour, the tired and weary group arrives at the camp. Mosha and Zofia have held each other's hands the entire way there, pulling each other along, not daring to speak as the soldiers march alongside them, looking determinedly ahead, clutching their guns close.

They stop at the entrance gate to the camp. People strain to see what's ahead but all they can see directly in front of them is a barren field with a huge sign with a skull and crossbones on it. The wording on the sign – in both German and Polish – states it is forbidden to enter the camp and that intruders will be shot without warning. There are several of these signs posted along the electric barbed-wire fence perimeter and one at every one of the eighteen guard towers.

6

Elsa Klein, thirty-two, lies in her bed alone but stares longingly at a newspaper cutting in her hand. The dawn light struggles through a tiny window, but Elsa holds the cutting up into what little light there is.

She looks stern; there's an efficient, manly air about her, despite her Aryan blonde hair styled in the latest fashion and her piercing blue eyes.

She is the *Oberaufseherin* (Senior Overseer) of the women's camp, so she has a room all to herself. The other female guards have to share two to a room. Some of them tried to complain when they arrived at the camp in October 1942 alongside the first female prisoners but soon learned to hold their tongue when they realised their accommodation was the equivalent of a five-star hotel compared to the prisoners' quarters.

Elsa looks around her room. It's sparsely furnished with a single bed, a nightstand with a radio on it, an iron washstand with a basin, and two chairs, just in case she wanted some company. In the corner is a wardrobe where her neatly pressed uniform hangs. She sits on the bed in her slip and underwear, confident that no one will bother her this early in the morning.

She looks down again at the clipping, announcing the promotion of Josef Hanke to *SS-Generaloberst* (General). She reads the words, even though she knows them off by heart. She sighs. Captain Hanke, her Captain, is being transferred to this camp. To her. She knows it's fate. They were meant to meet again.

Elsa thinks back to the first time she saw Josef, twenty years ago. She was a young, blushing girl of just twelve, on the verge of womanhood. He was already twenty-four and a leader of the Hitler Youth, about to transfer to the real army.

Elsa had been forced to join the female section of the Hitler Youth by her parents, who were stout supporters of the Nazis. But she found that she loved it, loved the strict regime, the ideals and the sense of belonging to something bigger than herself.

Later on, it became mandatory for all German girls between the ages of fourteen and eighteen to join the League of German Girls (*Bund Deutscher Mädel*, or BDM) but back then, Elsa was proud to be one of the first members.

She enthusiastically embraced the lessons on cooking, sewing, education and politics, all in line with Nazi ideals. She desperately wanted to become the mother of a future Third Reich leader, and she believed her dream would come true when she laid eyes on Josef Hanke. It didn't matter that he was already married when she saw him across the room at a Nazi Party political meeting.

Elsa closes her eyes and sees him again, as if it were only yesterday:

He is standing in his uniform with his back to her when she walks into the rally with her parents. But as her father, an SS-Obersturmführer (First Lieutenant), strides across the room to greet him and he turns their way, she gives an involuntary gasp. This is a real man, not one of the wimpy boys she sees at school or at the youth camp.

Josef greets her father warmly, and when her father introduces his family to him, Josef gallantly takes her mother's hand and kisses it – and then does the same to Elsa. She could have fainted – if she weren't made of sterner stuff. Members of the BDM don't behave that way. Her mother then drags her away to their table where she spends the rest of the night just staring at Josef, who is completely oblivious to her infatuation.

Elsa didn't see him again for five years but she never forgot his handsome face – or that kiss. When she got older, she volunteered with troop support, and at seventeen, they met again. He pretended to remember her; she just blushed when he spoke to her. By now Josef was married and had his own infatuation – with Mosha.

But Elsa knew none of this. And in his eyes, she was just a silly little schoolgirl, buzzing around him like an unwanted fly. But he couldn't swat her away – her father was now his superior. So, he smiled, said nice things and kept Elsa at arm's length, not knowing those kind words would lay the groundwork for a dangerous obsession years later.

Elsa opens her eyes, a huge smile on her face. Now, after all these years, he was coming back into her life, just like she knew he would. She kisses the clipping, then holds it to her chest. She sits there for several minutes, just thinking about Josef. For the first time since she arrived in the camp four months ago, she wishes she had some make-up.

In the BDM, the girls were actively encouraged to look pretty and wear lipstick and rouge. By all accounts, they should look their best if they wanted to be the perfect wife and mother. But here in this dreary camp, there is an unwritten rule. Look efficient. Look authoritative. Look menacing. Elsa knows she's not here to find a husband. Her main role in life now is to make sure these godforsaken little Jews do as they're told and do their work.

Still, she wished she could look better for Josef. An idea pops into her head. The warehouse where all Jewish goods that have been confiscated are held – surely there's lipstick in there. The smug thought leaves her head as soon as it pops in, replaced by another one: Can I bear to touch a lipstick that's touched the lips of a dirty Jew?

Elsa shudders at the thought. But her need to look her best for Josef wins out and she resolves to look for something that will appeal to him.

The siren suddenly blares across the camp.

It snaps her out of her daydream. She looks at the battered old clock on her nightstand. 5 a.m. Roll call is not due for another hour. The siren can only mean one thing: new prisoners.

She puts the clipping carefully away, out of sight for now. She walks over to the wardrobe and pulls out her uniform, a depressing black affair with the SS insignia on the arm. She pulls it on. There's no mirror in the room but Elsa knows how good she looks. She has to set the standard for the camp.

The siren sounds again. Elsa peers out of her tiny window and sees a crowd filing through the gates. She buttons up her jacket, takes a breath, heads outside.

7

The soldiers herd the prisoners through the gates and into the camp. They walk along a short road where they pass the SS quarters, which house thirty-nine barracks for the soldiers. They are sturdy, well-built structures, giving the prisoners false hope that they'll be living in something similar.

A man in front of Mosha and Zofia exclaims, 'They don't look so bad!'

Several of the soldiers nearby burst out laughing. One of them points to a little brick building, known in the camp as the Little White House. The soldier asks in a taunting voice, 'Maybe you'd like to live there?' More laughter.

Zofia whispers to Mosha, 'Who does live there?'

Mosha replies, 'Probably whoever is in charge,' just as the camp doctor emerges from the building. He walks over to the general, they exchange brief words and the doctor heads towards a large building in the distance.

The prisoners keep shuffling forward until they reach the prisoner pre-sorting area. Once there, the prisoners are split into two groups. Men on one side, women and children on the other. Soldiers snatch any larger possessions out of their hands, toss them onto an ever-growing pile. Some people resist, struggle to hang on to what is rightfully theirs – even if it's a kid's toothbrush – but are rewarded with a beating until they let go.

As the items start to hit the pile, a group of women appear and begin scooping them up by the armful. They totter away towards a huge warehouse beyond the prisoner area.

Inside the warehouse are sections for different things: shoes, clothing, toiletries, even money and artwork. All taken from the prisoners and never to be returned.

In front of the warehouse, just beyond the pile, are two booths, both manned by stern-looking SS soldiers. Men are lined up in front of one, woman and children in front of the other. The soldiers collect money, jewellery, anything expensive that's not already in the pile, ostensibly for safekeeping.

Johann Strauss's 'Blue Danube' Waltz plays over speakers. Mosha hums as she and Zofia reach the front of the line. Zofia grabs her by the arm. 'What are you doing?'

Mosha asks, 'What?'

Zofia lets go of her arm but tells her, 'Stop making that noise.'

'I'm just humming,' Mosha insists as she continues to murmur the tune.

'Stop. Please. Don't give them a reason to hurt you,' Zofia begs her.

But Mosha asks, 'How can anyone who plays this beautiful music hurt people? This was written to lift a nation's spirit. Maybe it's to cheer us up.'

Zofia looks around. 'There's nothing cheerful here.'

The soldier looks over his new batch of prisoners. 'Be quiet! Hand over any jewellery or money,' he barks. Zofia hands over her watch but doesn't reveal the necklace. She cries as she is forced to remove her wedding ring.

The soldier points at Mosha. 'You. What do you have?'

Mosha shakes her head. 'I think there's been some mistake. I think I'm in the wrong line.'

The soldier sneers at her, 'And what line should you be in?'

Mosha squares her shoulders. 'I am Mosha Gebert.' The soldier shrugs. 'Mosha Gebert, the pianist.'

He almost smiles. 'I don't care who you are.' He points at Mosha's hand. 'Now give me that ring.'

Mosha puts her hands behind her back. 'No, check your list.'

The soldier holds out his hand. 'Give it to me.'

'But it was my mother's ring!'

'I don't care. Hand it over. Now.' His raised voice attracts the attention of another SS soldier, who steps forward, points his gun into Mosha's chest. She reluctantly hands over the ring.

Now the soldier is really going to make her pay. 'Lift up your hair.' Mosha pulls her hair back to reveal nothing. This annoys the soldier, who was expecting to see something hidden, or at least a nice pair of gold earrings, but before he has a chance to make Mosha pay, another soldier steps up and shoves them forward.

A sense of foreboding washes over Mosha. She knows she will never see Zofia again. She turns and retches but there's nothing to come up. She swallows down the bitter taste of bile as she realises the captain is now watching her closely.

Mosha and Zofia stand with a group of women and children. Mosha steps to the side, approaches one of the soldiers and tells him, 'I shouldn't be here.'

'Get back in line.'

But Mosha is insistent. 'There's been a mix-up. Tell your commander who I am.'

The soldier shoves Mosha back in line but she stands her ground. The soldier grabs her, tries to drag her away, but Zofia clings onto her.

As they struggle with the soldier, Zofia's dress rips, the sun hits her necklace, almost blinds the soldier. He lets go of Mosha, grabs Zofia's dress and tears it wide open.

Zofia clutches her dress at the neckline but the soldier grabs her by the back of the neck, drags her across the room, throws her at the feet of an impatient captain who demands, 'What?'

'Show him!'

Zofia clutches onto her dress even tighter, earning her a rifle butt to the back of the head. The soldier hits her again and again and again. She's knocked unconscious as the soldier bends down, pulls open her dress.

The captain leans down, grabs the necklace. He holds it up; a greedy smile spreads across his face. The young soldier shakes Zofia until her eyes flutter open. She tries to focus, forgetting for a moment where she is. As she sits up, she realises what has happened and tries to scramble away.

The soldier grabs her ankle and yanks her back. Crying, she tries to grab at the captain.

'Take her away.'

Zofia screams. 'No! No! I'm sorry.'

As Zofia is hauled to her feet, Mosha steps forward to help her friend but she is pushed back in line. With a gun to her head, she can only watch as Zofia is led away towards a group of old and sick women.

One of the captains is approached by a senior officer. The captain salutes him and asks, 'The chamber?'

The officer shakes his head. 'No, I don't have anyone spare to clear it out. The last thing we need is that smell as the weather is getting warmer. They've only just cleared the last smell. I can't deal with that again.'

The captain nods in agreement. 'The execution pit then, sir?'

'Yes, that will have to do for now. Once these new prisoners have been processed, I'll have a lot of hands to put to work clearing the chambers, and then we can move some of the bodies from the pit to the crematorium too.'

Some of the prisoners have heard this conversation and can't stop the tears. Zofia and the group of rejected women are marched away from their loved ones and friends. There is no chance for goodbye, just tears and despair as everyone is too afraid to protest, fearing they, too, will be forced to join the end of the line, disappearing forever.

Zofia and the other female prisoners limp through the fields, past barracks and structures being built. They reach the execution pits on the other side of the camp, situated just beyond the crematorium and brick stack tower.

The soldiers stop them a few feet from a deep pit that already has bodies piled in it. Some prisoners weep, others are just too numb to react.

A few begin to say a prayer in unison: 'Hear, Israel, the Lord is our God, the Lord is One. Blessed be the Name of His glorious kingdom for ever and ever.'

Before they can say any more, a squad of SS soldiers run up behind them, stop in a line parallel to them. One soldier stands to the side, raises his arm, brings it down in a sweeping motion. 'FIRE!'

The soldiers open fire and bodies pitch forward into the pit.

Even though the pit is several fields away, the gunfire rings across the camp. Mosha, still waiting in the pre-sorting area, steps out of line, screams. A woman behind her grabs her, pulls her back in line. Mosha tries to twist away but the woman holds her still.

'Stay in line. If you want to live, don't move.'

Mosha weeps as she asks, 'Why? Why are they doing this?'

The woman whispers back, 'Because they can. If you want to stay alive, do as they say.'

'They will listen to me.'

The woman has no idea who Mosha is – or thinks she is – so she just shakes her head sadly. 'You are no one in here. Just keep your head down. Don't cause any trouble.'

'But they are killing—'

Mosha is hit with a soldier's rifle butt to the stomach. She doubles over in pain, staggers, grasps the woman's hand.

8

The women are steered inside a wooden hut. This is the women's bathhouse. The first room is dark and oppressive with no windows. Efficient but completely soulless, it sucks the warmth from the shivering prisoners as they cling to each other.

Here they are forced to strip naked. This is no time to be coy as the soldiers point their guns at them while laughing as the women slowly strip off. Once they are naked, they are pushed through to the next room, which has windows but is still just as depressing.

Mosha clings to the woman from the line. Until the smell hits her. The overpowering stench of Lysol makes her eyes water, and her hand instinctively covers her mouth as she gags.

The women are forced to walk through huge concrete tubs filled with the suffocating Lysol solution. The strong disinfectant stings their bodies, but if anyone whimpers, a guard leans across the tub, scrubs them with a wire brush.

This will be the only bath they'll get for weeks, although they don't know this yet. If they did, many would probably scrub themselves properly. In the coming days, they'll wish they could rub Lysol over their bodies to get rid of the dirt and fleas.

Once they've waded through the filthy water, they are forced to stand in a line on one side of the hut while hosed down with alternate hot and cold water. Tears mingle with the wetness that runs down their cheeks, drips off their shivering naked, red, raw bodies and pools at their feet.

After their 'purification', the women are each handed a bundle that contains a pile of rags that pass as clothes. Each bundle consists of either a skirt or trousers, a sweater, a blouse, one pair of underwear, stockings and a hat.

Mosha quickly wipes over her body with a tiny towel, stiffly pulls on the threadbare yellowish underwear, a blouse and skirt, all ill-fitting and now just as damp as her.

The sight of the women trying on their hats elicits giggles from the group. The hats don't match any of the other clothing. Some have huge bows, some have veils, and one or two even have ornate pins attached to them.

A woman helping guard the prisoners steps forward. She is one of the Block Elders – prisoners who have been hand-selected by the SS for various jobs around the camp and who form a kind of prisoner government. Some do this willingly, others under duress, but they all get privileges not afforded to regular prisoners. But working for the SS can have its own problems. The SS are not discriminatory in their beatings and even hardworking Block Elders can be on the receiving end of a baton. And while being a Block Elder might get you out of the backbreaking work in the fields and a little more food, it also means there are times they can help out their fellow prisoners.

But now this Block Elder needs to assert her authority over the new prisoners. She taps her baton on the door frame to get their attention.

'QUIET! You will dress in these clothes. You will all wear this every day. It will be your responsibility to wash your clothes. If you rip them or damage them, you will not be issued new ones. You will also be issued one standard pair of shoes.'

Once they are dressed, the women are ushered outside, which is just as austere as inside. Nothing beautiful or pretty grows here. It's a wasteland of misery.

But the spring sunshine feels good on Mosha's skin after the train ride and the oppressive dark building. For a brief moment she forgets that she's completely at the mercy of the younger male SS soldiers who are sizing her and several of the women up. The women huddle together, trying to help each other, even though they are completely at the mercy of these boyish soldiers who have barely hit puberty.

They are quickly marched away from the bathhouse and into the centre of Field V – the women's section of the camp. They stand in lines, like soldiers on parade.

In front of them is a raised platform. To the right of the platform is a semi-circular flogging table, officially known as the Block. Its nickname in the camp is, ironically, the Grand Piano. But it doesn't make sweet music. Instead, it elicits sounds of desperation and fear.

The women try not to look at it, but it draws their gaze, almost mesmerising them. Mosha can't tear her eyes away from it. She's never seen anything like it, but then, none of the women have.

A no-nonsense female guard walks among them handing out numbers printed on a piece of white linen. In a voice that carries across the compound she informs them, 'This is your number. You no longer have names. You will sew these onto your clothes.'

Another female guard follows behind like an eager puppy, this time handing each woman a badge hanging on a piece of string, also with their same number printed on it.

The guard's monotone continues: 'You will wear this around your neck at ALL times.' Mosha is handed her prisoner number – 5391. She turns the badge over and over in her hand before slipping her head through the frayed rope. As the badge drops against her clavicle, Mosha flinches. It instantly feels like a noose around her neck.

As the sun begins to dip on this long day, the women are directed into one of the twenty-two barracks inside Field V. Each building has just a handful of small windows that let in barely any light. Inside, Barrack 5 resembles a tomb, with the air so stifling.

The three-tiered wooden bunk beds are jammed in so close to each other, there's barely room for the women to move. There are no mattresses on most of the bunks, just hard wooden slats and two or three threadbare blankets for each bunk – as up to three women have to share each bed. The uncomfortable thin straw mattresses that had been on the bunks have been burned, thanks to the recent infestation of lice.

Mosha, entering with her group, gags from the overpowering stench. They stand near the door, unsure what to do. They slowly inch their way into the barrack, which is currently empty. But not for long as the weary women return from their workday.

They push past the new prisoners, heading to their bunks. These women are all dressed identically in a grey, shapeless uniform with blue stripes. Most of them are so skinny, the uniform just hangs off them. They ignore Mosha and the other women as they rush to grab their bowls and spoons to get ready for dinner.

But before they can head back out, *Oberaufseherin* Elsa Klein enters. The women instantly scramble to attention, stand by their beds. The newer prisoners follow their lead.

Elsa walks up and down the barrack, inspecting every little thing. She reaches the far end and walks back to where the new women are gathered. She informs them: 'I am *Oberaufseherin* Klein. I am in charge here. You will do everything I say.' She bangs a metal baton on one of the beds. Several women jump, look at the floor, their feet. Anywhere but at Elsa.

She strides between the beds again, spins to face the group of new women. Most of the women cast their eyes to the floor. One brave but foolish woman dares to look her in the eye. Elsa stops in front of her, smacks her baton into the woman's stomach. She doubles over in pain.

Elsa leans over her. 'How dare you look me in the eye? You are not my equal. Remember that.' She pushes the woman, who collapses on the floor, still struggling for breath. Elsa simply steps over her as she continues her welcome speech. 'These are the rules. You will rise at 5.30 a.m. You will have thirty minutes to get dressed and clean the barrack and have breakfast. Roll call outside will be 6 a.m. You will then join your work gang and will have half an hour to walk to wherever you are assigned. You are here to work. Either in the field or the factory. Work will be from 7 a.m. to 12 noon. Then lunch. At 1 p.m. you will go back to work until 6 p.m., or 5 p.m. in the winter. Evening roll call will be 6.30 p.m. Only when everyone is accounted for will you have dinner. Lights out at 9 p.m.'

The women don't move. They are transfixed through fear and a little bit of awe. Elsa finally adds to her captive audience, 'You will spend two weeks learning how this camp works and what your role is. After the two weeks' orientation, you will begin work.' Elsa turns and leaves.

As soon as the door bangs shut, the new women all scramble, push, shove each other to find a space, any space, to claim. Mosha approaches a lower bunk with two women on it. They look up at her, then reluctantly scoot over so she can just fit on the end.

'Thank you.'

She looks around and sees the other women settling into their new home. Some, like her, have been lucky enough to score a bunk, but several have to make do with the floor.

One of the women tells her, 'Put your stuff under the bunk to the left. The lower bunk is on the left, the middle bunk in the middle and the top bunk on the right.'

Mosha leans down and shoves her bundle under the bunk to the left. The woman adds, 'It's almost dinner time.'

Mosha asks her, 'How do you know—' She's cut off by a siren.

The woman grins and points to the sky. 'Everything around here runs to the beat of the sirens.'

There's suddenly a mad rush for the door. The woman tells her, 'Better get in line if you want some delicious slop!'

Mosha joins the women heading out of the door. She's swept up in the crowd as they file out into Field V. Hundreds of women join the queues for food in front of each barrack. A giant pot has been placed in front of each block, from which is being served some kind of slop. Overall, there are hundreds of starving women desperate for a morsel of food after a hard day's work. But this is also the time when they can socialise, get together and gossip.

The women chatter as they stand in line, swapping stories of what they've done that day or bits of news that they've heard. Mosha moves along with the line, just listening, horrified as she hears the women talk about what beatings they've had or seen that day.

Mosha finally reaches the front of the line. She holds out her bowl as someone dumps what appears to be soup in it. She also gets given a piece of bread that's as hard as a brick. She follows the woman in front of her over to another table, where she grabs a tin cup with a watery liquid inside it. She sniffs the cup and realises it's very weak mint tea. She takes a sip and tries not to spit it out.

The woman from her bunk appears at her side, steers her towards some of the women from her block who are sitting on the cold ground in groups in the field. It's eerily quiet as the women concentrate on eating and drinking.

The woman nods her head towards a group that Mosha recognises from her own barrack. They walk over and sit down. Mosha pushes the mess around and around in her bowl. It looks so unappetizing.

The other women watch her for a few seconds before her bunkmate jokes, 'It won't magically change into a steak no matter how much you stir it!' The other women laugh and Mosha smiles at them.

'How can you eat this?'

'Because we're hungry and if you don't eat it, you'll starve!'

Mosha tentatively takes a spoonful and struggles to swallow it down. She tries dipping the bread in it, hoping to soften it up, but it doesn't help.

Her bunkmate tells her, 'You'll get used to it. You have to. Once you start working you'll be so hungry at the end of the day, you'll eat anything.'

'Thanks! I think!'

The woman laughs and tells her, 'You're welcome! I'm Maria, by the way.'

'Mosha.'

The other women in the group introduce themselves: Eleonora, Paulina, Olena, Olga, Helena and Melania. But before they can get any further, the siren goes off again.

Mosha looks at her barely eaten food. Maria tells her, 'You can take it back to the barrack, it's okay. In the winter we're even allowed to eat in there. You are responsible for cleaning your own bowl and spoon, so if one of the Block Elders asks why you haven't eaten it yet, just tell them you are just going to clean it. But if you want to save the bread for later, tuck it inside your sleeve or in your shirt.'

Curious, Mosha asks, 'How do you clean the bowls? Apart from the showers in the bathhouse, I've not seen any water or sinks anywhere.'

Maria sighs. 'There aren't any. We get so little food that everyone eats up, unless they are really sick, so then we just wipe the bowls and spoons with whatever we have. In the winter it's easier as we can use the snow. But there's no fresh water here.'

'How do you wash every day?'

Maria laughs. 'We don't! If we're lucky we get a shower every few weeks and we can do laundry once every two weeks. But there's no water to wash daily.'

'And the toilets?'

'A trench at the end of the field. So try to hold onto it until the morning. You don't want to be trying to go in the middle of the night, especially in the winter.'

Mosha is aghast. 'That's inhumane.'

'What's inhumane is being on latrine duty and having to work with that smell every day.'

'I can't believe there are no proper toilets.'

'They don't care about sanitation. And don't worry, you'll only be on latrine duty as punishment. So just stay out of the guards' way and don't do anything to get them mad.'

The women jump up. One of them gathers all the tin cups, bowls and spoons and runs over to the cookhouse to hand them off.

By now the women have trudged back to their barrack, just as the sun finally sets. Lights around the perimeter of the camp flicker on. In the dark, the camp feels even less welcoming. The women enter their hut and get ready for the night.

Some just lie on their bunks, exhausted after the long day's work; some play cards; while others just sit together and chat. Mosha warily watches everyone, not sure what to do as Maria is lying on the bunk with her eyes closed.

After everyone has settled down, Mosha gets up from her bed. She approaches a group of women huddled together. Mosha clears her throat. They look up at her; several raise eyebrows. Mosha is hesitant at first but then just blurts out, 'I am Mosha Gebert. I'm looking for my sister and mother. They are Eva and Celina.'

The women all dismissively shake their heads, turn away from her. Mosha moves on. She goes over to some older women. Begins her spiel again: 'I'm looking for my family. Eva Gebert is my mother. My sister is Celina.'

One woman asks her, 'Where are you from?'

Mosha tells her, 'The Warsaw Ghetto.'

The woman gives her a sad look. 'Ask Irena over there. She's the camp leader and she came from Warsaw too and knows what happened to almost everyone.'

The woman points to Irena Olevsky, fifty-eight, once mildly pretty, now just plain with stooped shoulders. Despite her hunched-over stature she still commands the most respect in camp and is the one person everyone goes to when they want or need anything. It's not a role handed out by the Germans like the Block Elders but one that Irena naturally took over after being one of the first women transferred to the camp in October 1942 after being deported from the ghetto in Bełżyce. She's simply been here the longest and knows how everything works and has seen so many things she wishes she hadn't. It's given her a hardened shell – until you really get to know her.

Mosha approaches her with caution. 'I'm looking for—'

Irena cuts her off. 'Your family? So is everyone.'

Mosha pushes on. 'I was told you might know what happened to them.'

Irena looks her up and down. 'Maybe? What do you have for me?'

Mosha shakes her head. 'I don't understand.'

'Nothing is free. You want something from me, you pay for it.'

Insistent now, Mosha says, 'I just want to know if my family are still alive.'

Irena smiles at her. 'That's a big want. Worth at least three days' worth of bread.'

Mosha looks incredulous. 'Three days?'

Irena flicks her head at the other women. 'Look around you. What do you think most people here want?'

Mosha stares at her new campmates. Some stare back, hostile; others just offer a sad, knowing smile. This only spurs Mosha on; she doesn't realise yet that no one is special in this godforsaken place. In here, everyone is no one. 'You should want to help me. I am—'

Irena holds up her hand. 'I know who you are. And who your parents are. You're Mosha Gebert, the pianist. But you won't get any special treatment in here.'

'My parents?' The question hangs in the air. For the first time since they met, Irena looks uncomfortable.

'Dead.'

41

With one single word, Mosha's world comes crashing down. She sinks to the floor. Tears roll down her face but she doesn't cry out. Years of poise and detachment kick in and she struggles – and wins – to keep her emotions in check. 'How?'

Irena leans forward, as though she's about to spill the world's greatest secret. 'Shot. I heard the Nazis were looking for you, so they took your parents and tortured them. But they refused to tell them anything.'

Coldly, Mosha asks, 'And my sister?'

Irena takes a breath. 'Alive, as far as I know.'

'You've seen her?'

'No,' is Irena's disappointing reply.

A sceptical Mosha demands, 'Then how do you know?'

'She was taken away just after you.'

Mosha won't let it go. 'Do you know which camp?'

Irena shakes her head. But then reminds Mosha: 'Don't forget the bread.'

Surprised, Mosha queries, 'Bread?'

Irena looks her straight in the eye. 'I told you, no one gets special treatment in here.'

With a wave of her hand, Irena dismisses Mosha, who angrily spins, returns to her own bunk. She clutches the threadbare blanket as she lies down on her hard bunk. She closes her eyes, shuts out the noise of all the women around her.

9

Mosha is woken by what sounds like a rooster crowing. She sits up in bed, looking around, confused, as there's been no sign of any animals in the camp at all.

One more crow sound and then a woman's voice rings out across the barrack: 'Hello! Hello! This is Radio Majdanek.'

Mosha asks one of her bunkmates, 'What's going on?'

The woman lying next to her giggles and informs her, 'Oh, this is our daily wake-up call.'

Mosha replies, 'I don't understand.'

'Radio Majdanek. It's our way of getting news out there and lifting up spirits.'

Mosha listens as the voice continues. 'First, a warm welcome to all the new ladies that have joined us. Sorry about the overcrowded conditions, but it's the perfect way to get to know your new neighbours quickly and intimately! And now, time for the latest news from the past week. The past days have once again brought us many attractions – it's just a pity that they were mostly unpleasant.'

The voice belongs to Danuta Brzosko-Medryk. She and Matylda Woliniewska run the fictitious Radio Majdanek, bringing 'news' and hope to their fellow women. In a former life, Matylda was a message runner and underground newspaper distributor in Warsaw before her arrest in November 1942, and together, the duo gather the information to 'report' on daily life in the camp.

They have help with the daily broadcasts from political prisoners who were transferred to Majdanek from Pawiak, the notorious Gestapo prison in Warsaw, including Alina Pleszczynska, Hanna Fularska, Wieslawa Grzegorzewska, Romana Pawlowska and Stefania Blonska.

These women are fearless and strong in their political beliefs and enjoy poking fun at their captors. But they also reveal essential news. They let the women know what is happening in the men's camp and which SS guard is dishing out the most beatings that week. They appeal for donations to be brought to those most in need and shout out birthday wishes. Occasionally they also sing religious songs and hymns. And it's all peppered with gallows humour about the terrible conditions they face every day.

The 'radio studio' is located on the top bunk where Matylda and Danuta sleep. There's no microphone or transmitter, and this radio station only has a broadcasting range of one barrack.

But the women in Barrack 5 make sure they take the daily news with them and pass it along to all the women, whether they're working in the fields, the warehouses or the factories. By the end of the day, all the women prisoners at Majdanek have heard the radio's news.

And when they can, they try to pass any important information on to the men too.

Danuta continues with her broadcast as everyone in the barrack lies on their bunks listening intently. 'Just a reminder, ladies, the recent fashion trend is very unique. Everyone ought to wear a dress – blue and grey stripes only! Also, the stockings mustn't match – if one is black, the other must be beige, or, alternatively, one brown and one ash-grey. The currently fashionable shoes must be wooden with a very thick sole and a wretched paper top. All the hats must be replaced with all sorts of headscarves and cloths – as un-vivid and warm as possible. So much for the current fashion trends.'

Laughter ripples through the barrack as Mosha looks shocked. She asks, 'They can say that?'

Her bunkmate replies, 'The radio is always done before the guards come in. The Block Elders don't care about a report unless somebody says something mean about them, so we don't! Besides, most of the guards are too stupid to realise that words are our weapon. They don't understand the power of words. Their only power is pointing a gun or beating you with a baton.'

Mosha nods and listens again as Danuta adds, 'Two of the children in Barrack 17 are very sick with flu. They need extra clothes or blankets. So, if anyone working in the warehouse storage can grab anything that can help, please do! That's all for this morning. Have fun out there, ladies!'

Laughter again as the women begin to ease themselves out of bed, ready to face the day. The women chatter among themselves now. Mosha looks around at everyone, perplexed. After what she saw and went through yesterday, this morning almost seems like a holiday camp. But she'll soon come to learn this is the prisoners' way of coping with the atrocities they face each and every day.

10

Mosha stands in line with the other new women who have just arrived at the camp. One of the SS guards directs them over to one side of the field. Elsa suddenly appears, striding across the camp, a Block Elder running behind her, trying to keep up. She stops at the front of the first line. She looks the female prisoner up and down so intently the woman starts to shake.

Elsa says just one word: 'Field.' The Block Elder writes down the woman's prisoner number and then next to it: *Field*. At the next prisoner, Elsa states, 'Factory.' And so it goes on, line after line, 'Field, factory, infirmary, field, field, warehouse, factory,' until all the women have been assigned their new jobs.

Elsa briefly stops in front of Mosha. Looks her over. 'Field.' Mosha sags. She'd been hoping for an office job, maybe in the post office. She had been told those jobs were the most coveted. If she got one of those, she wouldn't be picking up rocks every day. Her valuable hands would be protected.

Before Elsa can move on, Mosha takes her chance and makes the foolish decision to speak. 'I'd very much like an office job.'

Elsa stops dead in her tracks. She can hardly believe her ears. She takes a step closer to Mosha, their faces just inches apart. 'You dare to question my decision?'

Mosha instantly apologises. 'No, I'm sorry. I don't mean to—'

But before she can say anything else, Elsa slaps her across the face. Hard. Several of the women gasp but keep their eyes averted, looking straight ahead, fearful they will get the same treatment.

Mosha is determined not to cry, even though her face is stinging. She then makes her second mistake. She looks Elsa in the eye. Elsa brings her hand up for another slap. Mosha cowers in anticipation as she blurts out, 'I'm a pianist. I need to keep my hands soft and flexible. So I can play again.'

Elsa slaps her again. 'Why should I care about your hands? You're never going to play the piano again.'

She raises her hand again and Mosha uses her last bargaining chip: 'I can speak German and English.'

Elsa sneers, 'I have enough women that speak German. I don't need you. And if you speak to me again, you'll be on latrine duty after you've worked in the field.'

Mosha tries to apologise. 'I'm sor—' This time it's not Elsa's hand that connects with Mosha – it's her baton to her stomach. The blow sends Mosha to her knees but Elsa is not finished yet. She hits her again and again, this time across her shoulders and back.

'What. Did. I. Tell. You.'

With every word comes another smack. Mosha tries not to cry out but can't help it. The pain is like nothing she's ever felt before. The blows suddenly stop and Mosha is yanked to her feet by one of the junior guards.

She has no time to check her injuries as Elsa tells the group, 'You have been assigned your jobs. You will join your work group immediately.'

She leans into Mosha, close to her ear, and taunts her: 'Have fun cleaning up everyone's shit for a week.'

Elsa saunters away from the group as the Block Elder looks at Mosha and shakes her head in disgust. 'It's your own fault. You're not to get any boots or shoes until after you've finished latrine duty.'

Mosha is close to tears but she won't give the Block Elder or the guards the satisfaction of seeing her weak or crying. She holds her head high and proud.

The women file back out of the warehouse and are split into their work groups: field, factory or office. The factory women are allowed every day to walk into the city of Lublin, where they work in the SS-owned factories and plants, mainly assembling and manufacturing weapons and ammunition for the war.

The women assigned to the 'office' get to spend their days indoors at the laundry, washing clothing and bed linen for the SS, or in the sewing workshops, mending the SS uniforms. Some will be in the kitchen, tasked with making the daily slop, while others will sort through the prisoners' belongings in the storerooms or help out in sick bays at the infirmaries. Any of these jobs is far preferable to toiling in the summer heat or the winter chill in the fields, collecting stones and rocks for the camp construction. The 'office' jobs are seen as a privilege and often come with perks. Not only do the prisoners get to be inside and are often sitting down but they also get to curry favour with the guards and, on occasion, are given extra food rations.

These jobs are highly coveted, but Mosha didn't want one for any of these reasons; she just wanted to safeguard her most precious possessions: her hands.

As Mosha and her group are marched the one kilometre to the field where they will work, she studies her hands. She wants to remember them as they are now – still smooth and unwrinkled. As she walks along, she practises imaginary music scales.

Is that awful female guard right? Will she never play again?

11

And so begins the arduous and exhausting daily life in a concentration camp for Mosha. It's the same thing day in, day out. Monotonous, tiring, with a fear that bubbles under the surface across the camp.

The loud siren screams across the camp at 5.30 a.m. every morning. The women wake to the blaring noise and rush to get dressed. It doesn't take long, as they're not allowed to wash and they have limited clothes. Most of the women, especially in the long, dark winter months into spring, sleep in all the clothing they have just to keep warm. So, when they wake in the morning, they just take off their sweater and swap it out for their hat. They know once they are in the fields or factories they will be worked so hard, they won't need to layer up to keep warm.

But at night in the barrack, which just has a small heater at each end of the room that barely exudes any real heat, they know they could freeze to death. The hut might have windows, but with construction on the camp so far behind schedule, very few of the barracks have real windowpanes that keep the heat in or the bugs out.

It takes the women just minutes to get ready. They file out into the chill morning air, thankful that at this time of the year, the sun is still hiding and they're not blinded by the rising rays as they wander out into the yard.

Mosha then lines up with all the other women to collect her breakfast – most mornings it's just a single cup of black fake coffee without sugar or milk. If the women are really lucky, they may get a piece of rock-hard bread left over from the day before.

As Mosha waits to be handed her pitiful tin cup, Maria nudges her and whispers, 'You'd think they'd want us healthy and strong for the amount of work they have us do.'

One of the other women in line pipes up, 'They don't care, they're probably rounding up a thousand more Jews in the ghetto right now. They won't stop until we're all in camps or dead.'

A few of the other women tut in agreement but no one says anything else. There is nothing else to say. Mosha keeps quiet and just peers into her cup at the dark brown liquid that sloshes around inside it. She takes a sip. It's a cross between bitter and tasteless, like everything else that's served up in the cookhouse. She forces it down. At least today it's warm; most days it's not.

Once breakfast is over, the women return to the field and line up between the barracks for roll call in lines of ten. They want to keep an eye on the guards, want to know where they are at all times. So, they stand to attention as SS guards walk between them.

Then comes the monotonous task of calling out everyone's name. This shouldn't take too long, but if one person takes too long to answer – or, heaven forbid, there is no answer – the guard will start again. Some days, roll call takes thirty minutes; other days it can take hours.

Mosha and her work group are marched out of the camp as classical music blares from loudspeakers mounted on special vehicles near the gates. Every day there is some kind of music in the camp.

In the mornings, they are sent out for the day with music playing loudly across the entire camp.

It's the same music through the same speakers that welcomes them back into the camp at the end of each day. Mosha quickly realises that music is an integral part of camp life and often finds herself humming along to tunes she's known since she was five.

But despite hearing this music playing every day, it doesn't make her happy, it doesn't bring the joy it once did. It's not long before Mosha – and all the other prisoners – know the music blares out at other times of the day – or even at night – whenever the Nazis want to drown out the sound of screaming or gunfire.

If the music starts up at night, the prisoners usually know that bodies are being transported from the gas chambers to the crematorium at opposite ends of the camp. No matter what time of day the gas chambers are used, the SS wait until the cover of darkness to load up the bodies onto a trailer and transport them over to the crematorium. The music is played to try to drown out the sound of the tractors pulling the trailers along past each field. But by now, the prisoners know exactly why the music is turned on at night.

The prisoners are also forced to sing every day out in the fields. Most of them can't hold a tune, but it's a form of torture inflicted by the guards. They laugh as they demand, 'Sing! Sing!' as the already exhausted men and women recite the lyrics of popular German songs the sadistic guards have chosen. It's not just a form of mental torture, it also intimidates the more insecure prisoners, who are left humiliated and degraded when they don't know the words and are repeatedly beaten until they learn them and know them off by heart.

The prisoners are all forced to sing on the march back into camp, which weakens them even more.

Mosha and the women work in a field alongside male prisoners – but they're separated on opposite sides of the field. They can see each other but they're not close enough to talk – or pass messages. They all dig to extract sand and stone. It's backbreaking work but no one dares stop for a second. Mosha only sings when the guards walk past; the rest of the time she pretends to mouth the words. A few prisoners don't mind singing to cover for everyone and keep the sound going, but Mosha has no interest in joining in.

The hours seem to drag by as the sun rises higher in the sky. When the prisoners are about to drop, the siren blares out. They have just one hour to walk back to the cookhouse, grab lunch and be back in the field before the siren starts up again.

The prisoners try to walk as quickly as they can to the cookhouse, but right now they're drawing on their last reserves. The fake coffee they had for breakfast hasn't given them any strength, and a morning in the fields has worn them down even further. But they conjure up their final bit of energy, knowing there's a meal waiting for them – if it can be called a meal.

Mosha lines up for lunch and doesn't even have the energy to look pissed off as she's handed a bowl of watery brown soup and a small piece of stale, hardened bread.

One starving female prisoner grabs an extra piece of bread. Within seconds she is being beaten by three different guards and then dragged away. Mosha glances her way. The guard catches her looking, waves his baton in her direction. Mosha looks away, concentrates on her own bread.

Mosha is soon back in the field as the afternoon sun beats down. She picks up huge rocks, struggles to move them. Drops one. An SS officer walks by, kicks dirt at her. Mosha is itching to retaliate, to throw dirt back at him, but she's been in the camp for less than three weeks and already knows the consequences of answering back or of even a wrong look.

The two weeks of orientation had taught Mosha and the new women all the rules they would have to abide by if they were to have any hope of making it out of there alive. The women work together to make sure everyone knows what to do and how to behave. But even after two weeks the women know any mistake – no matter how minor – could result in a beating or worse. Now they're trying to survive in the fields.

Mosha wipes the dirt off her face and out of her hair and bends down to pick up the next rock. She feels someone next to her and stiffens, expecting it to be a guard. But she's surprised to see that it's Maria.

'Stop working so hard.'

Mosha is puzzled. 'Why? If we don't pick up any rocks, they'll just beat us.'

'Keep picking them up, just do it slower. As long as it looks like you're doing something they'll pretty much leave you alone. There's no point wearing yourself out the first day!'

Mosha nods and smiles a thanks. And begins moving slower. She's still adding rocks to the basket nearby but she's now moving at the same speed as the more seasoned, in-the-know prisoners.

Several hours later the siren alerts them all it's the end of the workday. The men and women nod at each other across the field as Mosha and her work group walk back from the field, past soldiers. The women are first to leave the field – the men are held back until they've left so they can't fraternise.

Weary, barely able to walk in a straight line, the prisoners keep their heads down, anything to avoid confrontation. Many lean on each other for support as they take almost forty minutes to make it back to camp, over a distance that would take a normal, healthy person around twelve minutes.

They slowly file back into the camp and make their way to the barracks. But not Mosha. As she passes through the gate, the Block Elder pulls her to one side. 'Not you. Latrines. Now.'

Mosha is so tired she can't even protest. But as the Block Elder pulls her by the arm she manages to get out, 'Can I get some food?'

'No! This is a punishment. You can have something later.'

'But I don't have any energy right now.'

'You'll find it.'

The Block Elder accompanies Mosha to the latrine pit at the end of the field. The smell and sight of the unshielded sewage pits make her gag as they approach, prompting the Block Elder to tell her, 'You think it's bad now, wait until the middle of summer.' Mosha holds her arm over her nose and mouth as she looks at the human waste piled up in the pit, covered in flies.

Another Block Elder approaches and hands her a shovel – and a scarf to wrap around her face. She takes it gratefully, and after tying it tightly around herself, Mosha joins the others who are throwing dirt into the pit.

She keeps her head down, and even though it's a struggle with every scoop of dirt, she doesn't stop. Her body aches all over but she knows if she takes another beating today, it will be all over. She doesn't even notice when the sun completely disappears below the horizon.

An SS guard who has been lounging on a chair downwind from the pit stands and shouts, 'Enough for today.'

Everyone places their shovel in a pile at the side of the pit and starts walking back towards the barracks. Mosha is the only woman so she walks alone, until the Block Elder who gave her the scarf appears at her side. Mosha asks her, as her stomach rumbles, 'Can I get some dinner?'

The Block Elder shakes her head. 'The kitchen closed hours ago, there's nothing left.'

Mosha is close to tears. She's so upset she can't even get any words out as she knows this is going to happen every day for the next week of her punishment. She chokes back the tears for the second time today.

But suddenly she feels pressure on her hand. She looks down and sees the Block Elder has pressed a small piece of hard bread into her palm. The small act of kindness overwhelms her and tears slip down her cheeks.

'Thank you,' she whispers.

'Just keep your head down and stay away from Klein.'

Mosha nods through the tears. They have reached Barrack 5. The Block Elder squeezes her hand in reassurance. 'We're not all bad.'

Without thinking, Mosha – the girl who hates any physical contact – flings her arms around the surprised woman and hugs her. She returns the hug and the two women cling to each other for several seconds.

Mosha enters the barrack and makes her way to her bunk. It's past lights out at 9 p.m. so most of the women are already on their bunks, many of them asleep, worn out from the day. She sits on the end of the bunk, looks at her hands. Once delicate, her soft hands are now already rough, blistered and red-raw after just a single day's hard labour. She massages them as silent tears fall down her face. She angrily wipes them away and lies down on the edge of the bed. She's asleep within seconds.

12

The next morning, Mosha awakes to find Irena standing over her bunk. She's still a little groggy as Irena fires the question at her, 'Will you be joining us for prayer?'

'For what?'

'Prayer. We try to recite the Amidah in the morning and in the evening if we can, but at least once a day.'

'I don't think so.'

'I think you should.'

'Well, I don't really care what you think!'

Mosha's bunkmates, Maria and Paulina, look questioningly at Irena, who simply nods at them. They scramble off the bunk, grab their hats and make themselves scarce as Irena perches at Mosha's feet.

Mosha sits up, ready to face whatever Irena has to say. She's not in the mood to be chastised; she's tired, hungry and has very little patience today. But she waits for Irena to make the first move. Irena just sits there, looking at her. After a few minutes, during which Mosha is getting both more uncomfortable and more annoyed, Irena lays it out.

'You are probably going to be here a long time. Sure, you might get sick, you might die, but something tells me you're a survivor and you'll be around for a lot longer than some of these women. So, I suggest you do everything you can to fit in. And that includes joining our daily prayer.'

'Does everyone take prayer?'

'No, but—'

'Then I don't see why I should, just because everyone else is.'

'It will help you. It's just a short blessing. We don't have time for much else. Although many women here recite an individual prayer when they are in the field or the factory. It helps them get through the day.'

Mosha just laughs. 'Look around, Irena. Nothing is going to help us in here. I lost my faith in humanity a long time ago, and saying a few words each day is not going to help me.'

A sad look crosses Irena's face. 'You'd be surprised. Many of us thought we'd lost our faith by the time we arrived here. We've all seen horrible things, lived horrible things. But here, every day, we found each other, and that brought us back to our faith. And when we found it again, we also found hope.'

'Hope? Are you mad? There's no hope here. I've only been here a few days but I already know there's no hope. I know I will probably die in here. We all will. And no amount of praying is going to change that.'

'I feel sorry for you but if you choose—'

Mosha cuts her off. 'Well, I feel sorry for all of us. We didn't choose to come here. We didn't choose to be starved. Or beaten. Or humiliated. But it's happening every day. And saying a few words every morning or evening is not going to change that!'

Mosha's voice is now raised and several women nearby have heard every word. Mosha looks directly at them but they either turn their backs to her or just give her a cold stare. Irena notices this, like she notices everything.

She tries a different, gentler approach. She's determined to get Mosha to change her mind. 'Okay, forget about the prayer if that makes you uncomfortable, but you still need allies. You need the friendship of these women if you're going to survive. Do you want to be alone?'

'I've managed just fine on my own for this long. I don't need anyone else.'

'You've only been here a couple of weeks. You'll soon see that you need a friend or two here. We all support each other no matter what religion we are.'

'I've found that being alone means I don't get hurt or disappointed by anyone else. I only need me, no one else.'

'That's a sad way to live.'

'But we're not living in here, are we? We're barely surviving. Just leave me alone.'

Part of Irena knows that Mosha is right, she just doesn't want to admit it out loud. She reaches over and places her hand over Mosha's.

'Just know we are here for you, whether you like it or not.'

Mosha turns away and now refuses to even look at Irena. The older, worn-down woman gets up off the bunk and walks over to another fairly new prisoner. This time she gets a much warmer welcome, and the two women walk over to a group that has gathered at the back of the barrack.

There's not much room, but they cram in together, all holding hands as they begin to recite the morning prayer, Shacharit, led by Irena. More women who are still in their bunks also join in:

Hear, Israel! The Lord is our God, the Lord is one.
You shall love the Lord your God with all your heart, with all your soul, and with all your utmost.
Inculcate them in your children by reciting them while at home and away, when lying down and when getting up.
Bind them as a sign on your arm and let them serve as a symbol on your forehead.
Inscribe them on the doorposts of your house and on your gates.

The women just finish the prayer when one of the female guards bangs open the door, indicating it's time for roll call. The group quickly breaks up and the women file out to start another long, oppressive day.

As Irena passes Mosha, she gives it one last shot. 'Please, just think about it.'

Another woman walks by and says to Mosha, 'Baruch Haba.'

'Baruch Haba.'

'Baruch Haba.'

'Baruch Haba.'

Every woman that walks by Mosha gives her the same message: 'Blessed is the one who comes.'

Despite herself, Mosha gives a little smile – Irena is persistent if nothing else! She pulls on her hat and joins the end of the line to head out for roll call.

13

June 1943

Several weeks later, Mosha stands in line for morning roll call, now thin, gaunt, a hollowed look in her eyes. All the prisoners look the same, except a few newer detainees who look slightly healthier. But all of them shiver in the cold, despite it being the start of summer.

Oberaufseherin Klein marches out across the yard. She stands on the platform so everyone can see her. She casts a look over the assembled prisoners as she paces back and forth.

Elsa smiles, like she has some good news to share. 'We have a special guest arriving shortly to see you all.

SS-Gruppenführer Hanke is our new camp commandant. So, of course, we want to give him a very special welcome.'

She walks off the platform and begins to walk among the women, inspecting their uniforms. Most appear to pass her scrutiny; the ones that don't get a quick slap around the head – a short, sharp warning to tidy themselves up.

She ascends the platform once more to tell the women, 'We will greet Commandant Hanke in Field I. Move.' Elsa nods at the SS guards waiting at the end of the field. They take their place on either side of the women and escort them out of Field V.

The women arrive in the field a short time later. Field I is the largest of all five fields in the camp. It's the first – and best – constructed of all the prison blocks. There's not quite enough room to fit all 25,000 prisoners – give or take a few depending on the day – that are currently being kept in Majdanek, so there's some overspill into Field II.

The prisoners all stand in their usual lines as they wait for the commandant. And wait. And wait. They stand in the same spot for close to two hours. As the sun gets warmer and warmer, several prisoners faint. The minute they hit the ground, an SS guard rushes forward, grabs them by the arm and drags them away. Luckily for the guards, the gas chamber is just a short distance away, tucked behind the men's bathhouse next to Field I.

As the minutes tick by, more and more people begin to fall and are dragged away, until finally a car with Nazi swastika flags flying on the bonnet drives through the gates and pulls into the far end of the yard.

SS-Gruppenführer (Group Leader) Josef Hanke, forty-one, steps out of the vehicle. He still has his boyish good looks but now there's a mean streak that gives him a steely demeanour.

Elsa almost falls over herself to rush to his side. She's turned from an efficient, no-nonsense soldier to an over-eager puppy. But he brushes her off like a fly. Elsa trails after him as he stalks towards the women.

He will deal with them first. He has big plans for the male prisoners but to him, women prisoners are just an inconvenience. If they can't cook or sew, what's the point of having them here?

He turns to Elsa. 'This is all the women?'

Elsa can barely get her words out, she's so in awe of Josef. 'Yes, Commandant.'

Josef peers at the lines of women. 'And they all work alongside the men?'

Elsa has managed to compose herself. 'Yes. Some in the factory but most in the fields. They are strong enough. They work as hard as the men.'

Josef steps closer to the women. He walks up, then down a few lines, stopping now and then to take a closer look at a woman, but never, ever touching them. He stops so suddenly Elsa almost careens into his back. Josef inhales sharply.

He peers at Mosha. She keeps her eyes to the floor. He reaches out, gently raises her chin with his hand. Afraid, Mosha keeps her eyes downcast. Josef leans in close. 'Look at me.'

Mosha slowly raises her eyes, looks him directly in the eye. Josef drops his hand, steps back, almost as if he's burned. It's her! But how can it be? A million thoughts rush through Josef's head: This can't be real. How did she get here? Of course, she's Jewish. But the chances she's in my camp? It must be fate.

Mosha looks intently at Josef. She has absolutely no idea who he is. He opens his mouth to speak but quickly changes his mind. Confused, Mosha once again casts her eyes to the floor as Josef stomps off towards his car. As he climbs into the vehicle, Elsa catches up with him.

Josef's eyes are closed. He leans back in the seat, inhales sharply. He slowly opens his eyes, looks past Elsa toward Mosha. 'That female prisoner. Have her brought to me. Immediately.'

Flustered, Elsa complies, 'Yes, Commandant,' but then can't help but wonder. 'Can I ask why?'

Annoyed, Josef snaps, 'Just do it.'

'Yes, sir. What about the male prisoners? Do you want to address them?'

Elsa waits for an answer.

Josef briefly considers it, but his overwhelming desire to see – and touch – Mosha wins out.

'Tomorrow. At roll call.'

He slams the door, forcing Elsa to jump back out of the way. The car drives away towards the SS guard side of the camp as Elsa watches, a puzzled look on her face.

She stalks back over the women. Marches right up to Mosha just as the siren to start work begins. Mosha turns to follow the other women but Elsa yanks her back.

'Not you. Not today.'

Mosha's shoulders sag. What has she done now?

14

Mosha stands in the field as all the women around her march away. Some throw her pitying looks; others think she's finally getting what's coming to her. They all know she refuses to pray with them. They all know how unfriendly she has been since she arrived.

But making friends is the last thing on Mosha's mind right now. She's desperately racking her brain to try and think what she has done to upset or annoy Elsa Klein. She can't think of a single thing. Yet she knows the guards never really need an excuse to dish out a beating or a punishment. It looks like she's just unfortunate enough to be Klein's pet project this week.

Elsa stands in front of Mosha. She's mad as hell. 'I don't know why he picked you, but *SS-Gruppenführer* Hanke wants to see you.'

Mosha remains silent. Even if she wanted to say something, she wouldn't dare. Elsa walks around her, unable to see the appeal. She pokes Mosha in the shoulder. 'Well, why you?'

Mosha at last looks Elsa dead in the eye. 'I am Mosha Gebert.' The old confidence is still there; it was just locked away for a while.

Elsa snorts. 'Ha. You are prisoner 5391. You have no name here.' But Mosha stands a little straighter, a little prouder. Elsa shoves her towards the bathhouse. 'Get out. Go. Clean yourself up and be quick about it.'

Mosha runs over to the bathhouse but as usual there's no clean running water in here. She dips her hands into a bowl of brown, dirty water and splashes it on her face, making sure to keep her eyes and mouth shut tight. She takes the hem of her shirt and scrubs her face as clean as she can get it. She then tucks her shirt into her waistband. There are no mirrors in here so she has no idea what she looks like, but she dips her hands in the water again and runs them through her hair, hoping it looks vaguely presentable.

Just ten minutes later, a slightly cleaner Mosha is escorted across the dreary compound by a low-level SS officer. He directs her past the women's barracks, then the men's. Mosha wonders where they are going as they head past the gas chambers, then the SS sector and out of the compound, leaving the huge electric fence behind.

Now as they walk along the little road towards the main gate, Mosha is slightly ahead and the guard has his gun trained on her. If she steps out of line even an inch or makes a run for it, he'll have no hesitation in shooting her in the back.

They approach a little house. It looks tiny and basic from the outside, but to Mosha's mind, after being cramped in the filthy, bug-infested barrack, this seems like a palace. They stop in front of it and the soldier steps up and knocks on the door.

A voice calls out, 'Come in.'

The soldier swings open the door, pushes Mosha inside and closes the door behind her.

The inside of this tiny house is a five-star hotel compared to Mosha's new home. Curtains hang at the windows – this is no windowless crypt. Plush furniture, better cared for than anything else in the camp, fills the main room.

Mosha stands awkwardly by the door as Josef sits at a table in the middle of the room. It's barely breakfast time but on the table is a hearty meal of not-so-stale bread and porridge, while the smell of real coffee wafts across the room.

Music plays softly from a gramophone in one corner, while an upright Steinway piano sits in the opposite corner. It's seen better days but it immediately grabs Mosha's attention and she can't tear her eyes away from it.

Josef gestures to Mosha to come closer. She takes a few steps forward. He gets up, pulls out a chair for her. Mosha doesn't move. He gestures again. 'Sit. Please.' Mosha slides into the chair, desperate to avoid his touch, but Josef simply sits back down in his own chair.

He observes Mosha for a few moments. She refuses to look at him, although her eyes keep straying to the piano. Josef notices straight away that it's hooked her attention, but he's not going to let her near it just yet.

Instead, he tries a different approach to get her attention onto him. 'Would you like some food?' Without speaking, Mosha instinctively reaches for the plate in front of her, but Josef bangs the table with his fist. 'Not yet.' Mosha sits on her hands. She looks down at the plate.

Annoyed, Josef demands, 'Why can't you look at me?' Mosha finally looks up at him. Blank. Whatever Josef was expecting, it's not this. 'You really have no idea who I am?'

A defiant Mosha finally speaks, 'Should I?'

Josef laughs. 'I spent hours watching you. Hours and hours. I know who you are.'

Mosha breathes a sigh of relief. Finally. Someone knows her worth.

'I would know you anywhere. It's such a shame you don't remember me.'

Mosha searches her memories, trying to think of anything that might make her remember who he is. But still nothing. She doesn't dare tell him that when she was playing, she only cared about the music, not the fans or the people that came to see her. They were insignificant to her; it was only the music that mattered.

Josef begins to eat. He gestures to Mosha to do the same. She hungrily tucks into the meal. It's just porridge. But unlike the fake coffee or the watered-down vegetable soup, this is thick and actually warm. There's even butter spread on the bread, and as she takes a bite, all her senses suddenly come alive. After what she's been eating lately, it tastes like the most luxurious meal ever cooked. She hardly stops to chew the food and gulps down the hot coffee.

Josef stops to watch her, wipes his mouth with a napkin. Gets up from the table, walks around to Mosha. He drops the napkin over the food on her plate, then takes her hands in his. If he was expecting her to be pleased, he was wrong. Instead, she flinches at the contact.

But Josef doesn't seem to notice. Or if he does, he chooses to ignore it. He looks her up and down, almost like he's appraising her. Mosha squirms under the scrutiny. It's been a long time since anyone looked at her this way, but it makes her feel uncomfortable.

'You're not the beauty you once were, but those hands… No one could mistake those hands.' He raises Mosha's hands to his lips, kisses them. Mosha snatches them back, horrified.

Josef appears in an almost dream-like state. 'You remind me so much of my mother.'

'What?'

He carries on, 'She was a pianist too. Nowhere near as good as you but she played with the same passion you have. You are so like her.'

Josef walks over to his desk. He picks up a photo frame. Turns it around, shows Mosha a faded photo of a young woman – late twenties, dark hair, similar-looking to Mosha. It's Greta. She smiles in the picture as she holds hands with two young boys.

Josef caresses the photo. 'When we were children, she would play for us, and when she and my father held parties for the *Deutsches Kaiserreich*, I would hide on the stairs and watch.'

Her curiosity gets the better of Mosha. 'Does she still play?'

Josef is delighted she's showing interest in his mother and he smiles at her. 'No. She died when I was seventeen. I missed her music so much. But then I found you.'

'Me?'

'Yes. I first saw you play when you were just twelve years old. It was beautiful, so like my mother. The passion, the same love of music. I saw you every chance I got after that. I saw you in Berlin, Paris, even Warsaw.'

He walks over to the gramophone and turns off the record. 'When you played with the Philharmonic in Berlin, I waited many nights outside that stage door to see you. Yet you ignored me. Night after night. Do you remember now?' Mosha shakes her head. She has no idea of those long, lonely nights he spent standing in the cold, shivering, just waiting to catch a glimpse of her.

Mosha tries to explain: 'My mother. She wouldn't let me go to the stage door afterwards. She always took me straight home. She said I was too young to meet any men.'

Josef instantly forgives her. He'd forgive her anything just to hear her music again. 'It doesn't matter. You're here now. This is why you are here in this camp. You are here to play for me. Just me.'

But Mosha has no intention of playing her sacred music for this Nazi monster. She haughtily tells him, 'I don't belong to you and I'm certainly not your mother.'

Josef laughs as he walks over to the piano and lifts the lid. He gestures to Mosha to sit down on the stool.

She refuses. 'No, I'm not going to play.'

But Josef has seen her looking longingly at the piano. 'I know you want to. I saw how you looked at the piano when you came in. I know you want to touch it so badly.'

Mosha is embarrassed that he caught her looking. She denies it. 'I don't want to play!'

'Yes, you do. Just think back to those glorious nights in Berlin. Don't you want to feel that again?'

'I can't feel anything in this awful place. Music doesn't belong here. You use it to cover up screams when people are being beaten to death. I won't be part of that.'

'No, this music is just for me. Here in this room. It can be our little secret.'

'You're sick.'

'It will be just like before, at home in Baden-Baden.'

Mosha realises he's not talking about her anymore. 'I can't replace her.'

'Don't be ridiculous.'

'I won't play for you or anyone else in this camp.'

A battle of wills begins.

'You dare refuse me? Again. PLAY!'

Josef grabs Mosha, pulls her out of her seat and roughly drags her over to the piano. She fights him with every ounce of energy she has left. But that's not much, and Josef easily forces her to sit. 'You will play.'

'NEVER! Take your hands off me.'

'Play. Now.'

Mosha is furious. 'I will never play for you. Music is sacred. It should be played for joy, not in a place of death. I won't bring joy to such hateful people.'

Josef is genuinely perplexed at her choice of words. 'Hateful? We're not the monsters you think we are.'

But Mosha is adamant. 'You are killing innocent people. So many people.'

Josef's own anger kicks in. 'These people are not innocent. The 25-Point Plan is very clear. The good of the state before the good of the individual.'

'You're all monsters. You most of all.'

This is getting tiresome. Josef issues a threat: 'I can make life very easy or very difficult for you.' He saunters over to the table, grabs the bread. He offers it to Mosha. 'Don't you want to keep enjoying the finer things?'

She sneers at him, 'Not at this price.'

'You seem to have forgotten who is in charge here.'

Mosha's ego takes centre stage. 'And you seem to have forgotten who I am. I decide when I play and for whom I play.'

Josef tells her, 'We'll see. Take the bread, all of it, and sleep on it.'

Mosha rises from the stool. She walks past Josef, ignores his outstretched hands offering her the bread and goes out the door. Under his breath, Josef mutters, 'We'll see.'

He sinks into a chair, closes his eyes. He reaches out to a Volksempfänger radio on a side table by the chair. He turns it on to a Reich Broadcasting Corporation propaganda broadcast of Lord Haw-Haw.

A voice on the radio declares, 'There has been a breakdown of French resistance. France has laid down arms as the struggle has long been sustained. We should thank our gods for this victory and the relief it will bring for millions.'

Josef smiles to himself.

15

Elsa watches from the dark shadows as Mosha stumbles out of the front door of Josef's little house. Mosha wonders for a minute, looks towards the town of Lublin in the distance, then looks around and sees no guards anywhere. All it would take to escape right here, right now, would be the courage to run in that direction.

She weighs up her options but takes just a second too long as two SS guards appear in front of her. They each grab an arm and escort her back across the compound to the women's barracks. She tries to look back at the town, just sitting there waiting for her.

Elsa watches her leave before she turns and looks longingly at Josef's little house. She desperately wants to run to him, give him the comfort she's sure Mosha refused him. But for all her bravado, it's the one thing she's most afraid of – showing emotion, especially to a superior officer. Instead, she follows Mosha and her escort from a safe distance.

Mosha, unaware her every move is being watched by Elsa, walks onto Field V, but it's eerily quiet and empty as all the women are out at work. She stands there for a few minutes as the two guards chat between themselves before they notice her hovering nearby.

One asks her, 'Where do you work?'

'The fields.'

They sigh as one soldier gestures towards the gate. Mosha sets off in that direction as the two soldiers seem to be playing a game of rock, paper, scissors.

The younger, boyish-looking guard triumphs over the slightly older but still-barely-a-man guard as he imitates his rock smashing the other's scissors.

'Ha! I win! You get to walk to the field.'

The losing soldier looks more than grumpy as he trots to catch up to Mosha. As he reaches her, he uses the butt of his rifle to shove her in the shoulder. The force sends Mosha flying face first into the dirt. While she's down, he kicks her a quick, swift kick in the back. He looks over at the other guard and they give each other the thumbs up as Mosha struggles to get to her feet.

She is furious inside but knows if she says even one word to him, he'll hit her again. And again. And again. So, she keeps quiet, and despite the dull ache she now has in her lower back, walks as fast as she can to the field.

As she joins the other women they look at her quizzically but she just ignores them. They dare not ask her any questions for fear of a beating so they all just keep their heads down and get on with their work.

A few hours later as the lunch siren rings, Mosha prepares to head out with everyone else but a guard quickly stops her. 'Where do you think you're going?'

'Lunch.'

'Not for you. You need to make up the time you missed this morning.'

Mosha knows better than to argue back. At least she had a few spoonfuls of porridge this morning, which will see her through to dinner time, so she just shrugs and bends down to pick up the rocks.

The guard, annoyed at having to stay behind in the field and miss his lunch, kicks over the basket of rocks nearest to Mosha, sending them flying.

'Pick them up.'

Mosha doesn't bother to answer back, she just does as she's told as the guard then goes down the line, kicking over every basket until he reaches the end of the field.

Wearily, Mosha begins picking up all the rocks. The summer sun beats down and soon she's sweating from the heat and exertion. She stops, takes off her hat, turns her head upwards, wanting to feel the sun on her face. Just for a second she wants to believe she's standing in a meadow on a warm summer's day, enjoying the sunshine. For just a brief moment she wants to believe she's free.

And a brief moment is all Mosha gets, as the guard notices she's stopped work and starts running towards her across the field. Mosha quickly begins throwing the rocks into the basket. She avoids a beating this time but the guard stands next to her for the next five hours until the end of the day.

The siren finally sounds, and the women head back to the field for roll call. Mosha hangs back and walks alone. She is too tired to talk to anyone right now, even though she sees both Maria and Irena looking in her direction.

After roll call, the women stand in line to get their soup and bread. Irena taps Mosha on the shoulder but she doesn't turn around. Irena taps again. Mosha barely has the strength to speak but tells her, 'Later.' Irena accepts that and they fall into an uneasy silence.

Lights out. Mosha is lying on the bunk, desperate to sleep, but the women are too inquisitive and they crowd around her. Irena pushes through the crowd. 'Well?'

Mosha hesitates but decides there's no point trying to keep secrets here. She tells the waiting women, 'He wanted me to play for him.'

Irena asks what everyone is thinking: 'And? Did you?'

Mosha sighs and admits, 'I refused.'

Irena asks, 'Why?'

Mosha tells them simply, 'I will never play for him. Or any other Nazi.'

Before Irena can ask another question, a thin, dark-haired woman pipes up and tells her, 'You're a fool. What does it matter?'

Indignant, Mosha replies, 'Of course it matters.'

But the thin woman presses on. 'No, it doesn't. They don't appreciate it anyway so who cares?'

Mosha fights back angrily. 'You are not a musician. You will never understand. None of you ever will.'

Irena gently tells her, 'Then make us understand.'

Mosha tries to explain, more calmly now. 'Music is sacred. It should bring joy and happiness. Besides, I will be the one to decide who listens to me. People used to pay great money to hear me play.'

Another woman scoffs. 'How many years ago was that? You're not special here, no one will pay you here.'

Mosha retaliates, 'I don't care. I won't play for that man.'

The thin woman asks, 'But maybe this commandant is different?'

Mosha gives a brittle laugh. 'He might be different but he's worse. Much worse.'

Several women ask in chorus, 'Why?'

Mosha makes a point of looking each of them in the eye before saying, 'I looked into his eyes. There's nothing but evil there.'

Irena shakes her head. 'You need to look inside yourself. This will bring you nothing but pain.'

Mosha doesn't want to explain herself any more. 'Just leave me alone.' She lies back down on her bunk, turns away from the other women. As they drift away, she practises the scales on the 'air piano'. Maria watches Mosha and just shakes her head sadly.

There's a commotion as the lights flicker back on and several soldiers enter the barrack. They are carrying several baskets of bread and extra blankets. They hand them out to the women, who all look at each other, stunned. A young SS soldier puts a huge hamper basket down on the floor. 'A gift. From Commandant Hanke.'

The women greedily grab them from the soldiers as Mosha pushes her way through the crowd of women. Annoyed, she tells the soldiers, 'Take them back.'

Several women turn and glare at her as the thin woman declares, 'I'm keeping this blanket.'

Another woman tells her, 'We need this food!'

And even Irena insists, 'You can't send it back.'

Mosha tries to explain to them, 'He's doing this to make me play.'

But they still don't understand – or care – as Irena asks, 'What will it hurt to just play for him? Look at all the bread we can have. We need it.'

But an outraged Mosha tells the soldier, 'Tell Commandant Hanke that an extra blanket and a bit of bread won't change my mind. He can't buy me or my hands. This is pointless.'

Both the soldier and Irena shrug at her. Irena picks up a blanket and offers it to her as the rest of the women chatter happily and grab what they can.

Completely livid, Mosha spins on her heel and, empty-handed, heads back to her bunk.

16

Several days later, the women sit outside on the grass by their barracks to eat a meagre lunch. SS guards patrol the area, keeping an eye on them at all times. Mosha sits with her group, a shadow of her former self. She's painfully thin and even more gaunt.

One SS guard walks past, casually tosses a package into the middle of the group. 'From Commandant Hanke.'

The women smile, scramble to open the package, ripping open the faded brown paper. 'It's just like Christmas!' one of them quips.

Inside is yet more bread. Several different kinds of bread. Not the usual hard, stale bread they are force-fed every day. This bread is still warm and soft and it smells divine. The scent of freshly baked bread almost sends the women into a state of heavenly rapture.

They quickly share it around, eager to eat it before it gets cold. Maria offers a piece to Mosha but she refuses and turns away, disgusted. She keeps her back to them as they moan with delight at having such a decadent meal.

A young girl, Lotte Schiessel, eighteen, rushes over. She's a new prisoner; she still has curves and her hair still shines. She also bears a striking resemblance to Mosha's student Anna. She stops in front of Mosha and waits. And waits. When Mosha continues to ignore her, she tentatively asks, 'Are you Mosha Gebert?'

Mosha looks her up and down. Painful memories of Anna swim to the surface but Mosha pushes them down. She doesn't want to show any weakness in front of the other women, and especially not the guards.

She swallows, checks herself. 'Yes, I am.'

Lotte excitedly tells her: 'I want to start a choir.' Mosha just looks at her. Lotte pushes on. 'Irena said you would help.'

Mosha looks over to Irena, who just raises her eyebrows. 'What else did Irena say?'

Lotte excitedly continues, 'That you are a great musician and no one else here can play like you!'

Mosha allows herself a little smile, a smile that doesn't go unnoticed by Irena. 'Well, that is true!'

'So will you?' asks Lotte.

'Will I what?'

'Teach me!'

Mosha shakes her head. 'You don't want me as a teacher.'

Lotte is curious. 'Why not?'

'My last student… It doesn't matter.'

But Lotte is determined to get Mosha on her side. 'But everyone talks about you. About how much happiness it brings you. I just want to feel that.'

'I'm sorry, I can't. Music and singing are forbidden unless ordered by a guard. I don't want to get anyone into trouble. I don't want to be the reason that someone gets a beating.'

'But you wouldn't be. I know the risks. I love music and singing but I don't know very many songs. I just need someone to help me.'

'I said no!'

Angry, Mosha throws a look over at Irena before she gets up and walks away. The sirens ending lunch begin to blare as Lotte is left standing on her own, completely dejected. Irena walks over, puts her arm around Lotte, gives her a little squeeze. Irena tells her, 'She'll come around, just give her some time.'

As the women head back to work, Josef is safely ensconced inside his little house, seated at his desk, flicking through a pile of paperwork. Even though he's the only one there, he wears his full uniform. Always ready to stand to attention. A knock at the door pulls him out of his deep concentration.

He barks, 'Enter!'

Elsa sweeps into the room. She stops in front of the desk, waits for Josef to look at her. After several seconds she thrusts several sheets of paper at him. 'The list of new *häftlings*,' (prisoners).

Josef takes the papers. Flicks through. Stops on one page – a name catches his eye: Celina Gebert. He looks up at Elsa. 'This group. Have they arrived yet?'

Elsa replies, 'No. We expect them this afternoon.'

'I want one of them bought to me as soon as she's been processed.'

The urgency in his voice intrigues Elsa. 'Which one?'

Josef almost whispers her name: 'Celina Gebert.'

'Gebert?'

The bitterness in Elsa's voice causes Josef to stop flicking through the list and look at her. 'Yes.'

Despite the sternness in his tone, Elsa cannot help herself and blurts out, 'What is your fascination with her?'

Josef coldly asks, 'Who?' although he knows exactly who Elsa is referring to. He looks at her, daring her to question him.

Elsa takes the bait. 'That stupid little pianist.'

Josef holds his anger in check. 'I saw her play many years ago. She is one of the finest pianists in the world.'

Elsa exclaims, 'But she's Jewish! How could you—'

Josef bangs his fist on the table. Elsa immediately clamps her mouth shut. She's never seen him this angry. Yet his voice is calm as he instructs her, 'Just bring her sister to me.'

Afraid of him, Elsa replies, 'Of course.'

Now she's been reminded of her place, Elsa is rewarded with a smile from Josef. He walks her to the door, opens it. She has no choice but to leave. Josef shuts the door behind her, walks back to his desk, picks up the sheet of paper, underlines Celina's name again and again.

17

It's early evening as the women finish up their sparse, tasteless meal. Music starts blaring over the loudspeakers. By now they all know what this means at this time of the day. Irena drily comments, 'The new meat is here.'

Mosha throws her a dirty look. 'Stop calling them that.'

A defiant Irena retorts, 'Well, it's true. They treat us like cattle. This is a slaughterhouse.' Mosha stands up, walks away from the group.

She heads towards the barbed-wire fence between the barracks. She knows it will be a while before the new prisoners are processed but she tries to catch a glimpse of them, even though she knows they are too far away. Every time a new group comes in, Mosha patiently waits, hoping her sister will be with them.

Most of the prisoners here already were brought in together as families after being rounded up and taken from their homes. They travelled together on the death trains, believing they would be kept together, before being separated once inside the camp. Word still manages to get around the camp when a prisoner is executed, so families know they've lost their loved ones. But Mosha is one of a handful of women that arrived at the camp alone and doesn't know what has happened to her sister.

Every time the music starts up during 'leisure time' she heads towards the barbed wire. She's joined by a few other women, who sit on the ground and patiently wait to see what new prisoners have arrived. They won't see them until they've been searched, stripped and are heading to the bathhouse.

Mosha and the women wait, hoping the prisoners will be processed before lights out. Thankfully, the summer sun stays in the sky a little bit longer, giving them a few more precious minutes of waiting.

Mosha has almost dozed off when she hears a commotion on the other side of the fence. She jerks awake and sees thirty or so women being marched along towards the bathhouse. She's conscious of not getting too close to the fence for fear of angering the guards, but moves a little forward, straining to see in the low light as the sun begins to set.

As the naked prisoners stand in line waiting to head into the hut, Mosha scans the line. She moves slowly, closer and closer to the fence, unsure if she is really seeing her sister about halfway down the line.

'Celina! Celina!'

A guard rushes over, grabs her, tries to drag her away, but Mosha, without thinking, grabs the fence. Luckily it's only the perimeter fences that are electrified. Desperate, she struggles with the guard, oblivious to the consequences of defying their rules. The guard pries her hands off the fence. Mosha is still fighting him when another guard runs over. They pull Mosha backwards away from the fence as a young woman in the line turns to see what all the commotion is.

It is Celina.

She sees Mosha, takes a tentative step out of the line, but a guard quickly shoves her back. She cries out to her sister, 'Mosha!' Celina tries to get around the guard but he points his gun at her. Without thinking and purely on instinct she pushes it away. But before he can pull the trigger, Elsa suddenly appears and quickly steps in, standing in between the soldier and Celina.

The guard drops back but keeps his gun raised. Elsa turns to the soldier, who is not much older than a schoolboy. She pushes his gun down to his side. He looks confused but doesn't dare question Elsa's authority.

Elsa turns and looks Celina up and down. It's a look of disdain but Celina doesn't notice, she's still trying to look for Mosha. Elsa taps her on the shoulder. 'You are Celina Gebert?' It's more of a statement than a question, but Celina is rooted to the spot, unsure what to do. She desperately wants to see Mosha but has a gut feeling that something is off.

Elsa physically pulls her out of the line, shoves her in the opposite direction to where she wants to go. Elsa takes her into the bathhouse ahead of the other prisoners and orders her to wash. Celina splashes some dirty water on her body before Elsa hands her a dirty towel to dry off. Celina barely has time to rub herself down before Elsa grabs her by the arm again and steers her to a pile of clothes just inside the door.

Elsa picks through the pile and tries to select the least stained, least shabby. She knows how Josef will react if she presents Celina to him looking like a homeless gypsy. Celina pulls on the clothes. They are a little too big for her but she tucks in the blouse and smooths out the skirt.

Celina finally finds her voice. 'Are you taking me to my sister?' She's rewarded with a harsh laugh from Elsa. Celina then asks, 'Where are we going?'

Elsa tells her, 'Be quiet!' as she marches her past the bathhouse and across the compound.

Celina takes a quick look in the field where she had seen her sister, her eyes try to adjust to the dark as she searches for any sign of Mosha, but she's no longer there. Was it just a mirage? Was she hallucinating?

Inside the women's barracks, Mosha lies on her bunk, frozen. Her left eye is swollen and her lip is split from the several punches she received from the guard as she tried to get away, to run to her sister. The other women crowd around her. Helena tries to wipe away the blood on her lip, but Mosha just swats her away. She wants to be left alone.

Irena pushes through. 'What's wrong?'

Mosha is silent, she can't speak. Or rather, won't speak. Maria pipes up, 'She hasn't said a word since the guards dragged her in here.'

Irena grabs Mosha, shakes her, trying to bring her out of her stupefied state. Mosha finally looks up at her. Her mouth moves but nothing is coming out. Irena shakes her again.

Finally Mosha finds her voice. 'She's here. She's here,' is all she can say.

'Who?' Irena asks. When Mosha offers no reply, she asks again, more forcefully, 'Who? Who's here?' Irena looks around at the other women. They shake their heads. Irena grabs Mosha by her shoulders just as she comes out of her fog.

'Celina! I saw her.' The women exchange disbelieving glances, sure that Mosha is now hallucinating from sheer exhaustion. 'It was definitely her. You have to believe me.'

The women exchange knowing glances. They've all thought they've seen things inside the camp at some point. A lack of food, exhaustion, dehydration – all these things make them have their own fantasies and visions from time to time. But they usually realise pretty quickly that they are seeing things not really there, while Mosha is adamant her sister is now in the camp.

She sits up, wild-eyed. 'I'm not seeing things. I'm not.'

Irena tells her gently, 'The odds of it being Celina are very slim. It's been months since you saw her. If the soldiers were at your house that day, they probably took her too. And she would've been brought here too, probably on the same train.'

But Mosha insists, 'She could've got away. Or she could've been taken to another camp. I know what I saw.'

Irena realises she needs to calm Mosha down; her demeanour is starting to unnerve some of the other women.

She grabs an extra blanket from the next bunk over; the woman goes to protest but keeps quiet at Irena's stare. She lightly wipes Mosha's face before throwing the blanket around her. For once, she doesn't protest at having an extra blanket, and for once, does as she's told.

Irena turns to leave and she grabs her wrist, pulls Irena in close to her. 'It was her. My sister has come back to me.'

Irena pulls the blanket closer around her as Mosha closes her eyes and, for the first time in years, falls asleep with a smile on her face.

18

Later that night, Celina sits at the dining table in Josef's hut. She looks around, not sure why she's there, but also fascinated by her surroundings. The hut seems overly opulent to her after weeks of being kept in austere holding camps.

It's been a while since she sat at a table or saw curtains. Everything feels foreign, not quite real. Josef steps out of the shadows at the end of the hut and walks slowly towards her. He gestures to a plate set out in front of her.

Celina looks down, surprised to see a meal laid out before her. She'd been so preoccupied with taking in every little detail in the room, she hadn't even noticed the food in front of her. Now aware of it, the aroma of the meat penetrates her senses. Her stomach rumbles. Celina grabs at the food with her fingers, ignoring the cutlery.

Josef nods, pleased with how things are progressing. He strolls over to his gramophone, puts on some classical music – Beethoven's 'Waldstein' Piano Sonata. It's a mysterious slow movement, before the final movement takes flight with a glorious soaring theme. He just knows that Mosha would appreciate it, and hopes Celina will too. But he has no idea that Celina doesn't have a musical bone in her body. She doesn't care about music – or Beethoven – the way Mosha does.

She's oblivious to anything but the food on her plate.

Across the camp, Mosha lies on her bunk, now wide awake. Sleep was fleeting this evening. She tries to occupy herself by practising piano scales but she's too restless. She gets up from her bunk, paces up and down. Several women call out, 'Get back into bed. You're keeping us awake!'

Mosha sits back down on her bunk. It's 2 a.m., but the door of the barracks opens. An SS soldier steps inside. He calls out, 'Prisoner 5391.'

Mosha jumps up, runs to the door. 'Yes?'

The soldier gestures to the door, indicates she needs to leave. Mosha doesn't need to be told twice; she doesn't even complain when the soldier pulls her out of the barrack and pushes her across the compound.

After walking past three fields, Mosha realises they are heading towards Josef's house and possibly a reunion with Celina, and she breaks into a run. Taken by surprise, the guard struggles to keep up with her as she takes off across the compound. It's pure adrenaline that's spurring her on, faster and faster. But she has to stop when she reaches the camp gate. Completely breathless and feeling dizzy, she turns to see how close the guard is. She's rewarded with a slap around the face, which leaves her struggling to catch her breath even more. Yet, she doesn't care. The only thing that matters now is seeing Celina.

The guard signals for the gate to open and then grabs Mosha in a vice-like grip and marches her through the gate and down the road to Josef's house. But he makes the mistake of letting her go as they reach the front door. Before he even has time to knock, Mosha bursts in. And suddenly stops.

Celina is in Josef's arms as they dance to the music. She looks uncomfortable and stiff as Josef sweeps her around the room. A grimace is set on her face, while Josef, in complete contrast, has a dreamy, faraway look in his eyes.

Seeing Mosha standing in the doorway, Celina breaks free from Josef's grasp, runs over to her sister. They hug, weep, cling to each other. Josef lets them have their little moment before he strides over, pulls them apart. Celina fights, tries to keep a hold on Mosha. But Mosha knows. She takes a step backwards, untangles herself from Celina's grasp while Celina wriggles to free herself – but there's no escaping Josef's firm grip.

Mosha looks questioningly at Josef. She knows how his mind works but understands they have to play this game of cat and mouse.

She's the only one in the entire world who can speak to him this way: 'What were you doing?'

Josef smirks. 'Enjoying each other's company.'

Mosha wants to end this sickening game. She steps forward. Just one step and Josef twists Celina's arm; she cries out. Mosha takes another step; he twists even harder.

'Leave her alone!'

Josef reveals his endgame: 'Play.'

Josef twists again. In retaliation, Celina kicks Josef, hard, in the shin. Surprised, he lets go of her arm. Mosha rushes forward to grab her sister but Celina is in full fight mode. She punches Josef repeatedly in the chest and about the face. But she's so ineffectual, he starts to laugh, infuriating her even more. Fearful of what he will do, Mosha pleads with Celina, 'Stop it!'

The noise brings two SS guards, who burst into the hut, guns poised. Josef is furious at being humiliated in front of his own guards as Celina continues to pound on his chest. Josef gestures to the guards, who each grab a sister. With the threat of a gun in her face, Celina finally calms down. But while her fists might now be restrained, her tongue certainly isn't. 'Coward,' she spits out at Josef.

He ignores her, stands directly in front of Mosha. Waits. Anyone else would be intimated, but not her. She knows what he wants but even the threat to Celina won't force her to comply.

'PLAY!' Josef almost screams in her face.

Mosha looks past Josef at her sister. Celina shakes her head. The sisters are in this together. And Celina knows her sister better than anyone and has already sized up the situation and quickly grasped the dynamic of this sick, twisted relationship. But Josef also notices the look between them, covers the room in two seconds and grabs Celina.

'Don't you dare play for him,' Celina warns Mosha as she turns to face Josef. 'You can threaten me or beat me, but it doesn't make you any more of a man.'

Mosha implores her, 'Celina, stop. Don't antagonise him.'

But Celina is adamant. 'No! He doesn't deserve you.'

'How dare you!' A furious Josef raises his hand, slaps Celina across the face. Celina begins to giggle, which prompts another slap, harder this time. As Celina clutches her face, Mosha can bear it no longer.

She approaches the piano like an old lover she hasn't seen or touched in years. She doesn't want to do this, but if she can stop Celina being hurt, she will. But before she can open the piano lid, Celina rushes over, grabs her hand, pulls her away.

Mosha looks at the red mark on Celina's face and tenderly touches it. Celina leans into the caress, smiles at her, whispers, 'It's okay.'

Celina turns to Josef. 'She will never play for you.'

Josef asks, 'You think your sisterly bond and affection gives you the upper hand?'

Celina's response eerily echoes the words Mosha threw at him in the same room months ago. 'No. I think you're a monster who doesn't understand that blood is thicker than water.' She taunts him: 'I have something with her that you can never have or understand.'

Josef instructs the soldiers, 'Tell *Oberaufseherin* Klein no food for any of the women.'

Mosha runs to him. She suddenly realises it's not just about her or Celina anymore – it's about all the women. She knows now that he can punish them all as well as reward them. She begs, 'Punish me, just me. Not the others.'

But Josef tells her, 'Too late.'

Mosha hesitates, then drops to her knees. 'Please, just me. None of the other women have done anything wrong.'

Josef hesitates for just a second. 'NO! Every day you refuse to play, you all go without food. No more packages. Take away all their blankets too.' He turns to the guards. 'Get them out of here… No, wait.' Everyone in the room looks at him.

Josef tells the guards, 'Parade. Now. Wake up *Oberaufseherin* Klein. And get all the women up.'

One of the soldiers dares to question him: 'But sir, it's only 3 a.m.'

But Josef is determined. 'I don't care. Do it. And take these two with you.'

The soldiers salute him before they grab Mosha and Celina, shoving them out the door. Josef walks over to the gramophone, turns the music up and stands in the doorway, and begins to laugh.

19

The music from Josef's hut is so loud it drifts over the camp as the soldiers drag Mosha and Celina into the middle of the yard.

Mosha turns to Celina and hisses, 'You shouldn't have done that.'

An indignant Celina hisses back, 'I just stood up for you and you're mad at me?'

The pair go back and forth:

'I didn't need you to step in. You've just made things worse.'

'I was only trying to help.'

'Just do as you're told in future.'

'Don't tell me what to do. I'm not your assistant anymore.'

'Think before you act. This is not home.'

'Don't you think I know that?'

Mosha hesitates, 'Home…'

'What? How can you think—?'

'Quiet!' A soldier approaches them, points his gun. Mosha reaches out to touch Celina's shoulder but she shrugs her off.

Inside the barracks, guards walk between the narrow aisles, shouting as they push women off their bunks. They snatch their blankets from them as they bark orders. 'Up! Everyone up. Roll call now.'

The women grumble but can do nothing except follow orders. They scramble to put on shoes, threadbare cardigans, anything to keep warm, as they are forced out of the hut and into the compound.

The women stand in lines, shivering in the damp, cold night. Mosha and Celina stand on their own to one side, guarded by two soldiers. Elsa, next to them, glares, furious at being woken. Dirty looks are also thrown their way as Josef strides across the yard, climbs a few steps onto the platform so all the prisoners can see him.

Josef beckons to Elsa. She roughly pushes Mosha and Celina to the front of the yard. Celina looks at the ground but a still-defiant Mosha looks straight ahead at her campmates as Josef gestures to them. He raises his voice to make sure it carries through the cool night air. 'I want you all to look at these two.' He pauses as the women strain to see. 'It's because of them you are not going to get any food today. Or tomorrow. In fact, you will not be fed until Mosha Gebert does as she is told. The longer she defies me, the more everyone in this camp will suffer.'

A murmur runs through the compound. No one dares yell out or say what they really feel, but the tutting and sighing of several thousand women rumbles through the yard. Many of the women look outraged.

Josef continues, 'Take a long, hard look. Now everyone, get to work.' He gestures to a guard, who runs towards the gates. The gates swing open as the guard enters a hut next to the gate. Music blares out over the loudspeakers. The women look at each other, confused in the dark of the early morning.

Josef yells, 'NOW!' The women trudge through the gate, none of them properly dressed or ready for the workday. Many of them stare daggers as they pass Mosha and Celina. Elsa pushes the sisters to join the end of the line. Celina reaches to hold Mosha's hand, but Elsa spots the gesture and smacks Celina's arm with a baton. Luckily, it's not broken, but the pain leaves tears streaming down Celina's face.

Elsa watches as the women walk towards the field, a smug look on her face.

By late morning the women are exhausted. They have been working since 4 a.m., digging for stone to build the new crematorium or making ammunition in the factories. They have worked non-stop alongside the men, who were puzzled to see them without their hats or thin sweaters. They were not allowed any breakfast and were forced to work through without their pitiful cup of bitter coffee and piece of ersatz bread.

A siren signals lunch. Everyone stops, downs tools. Bullhorn in her hand, a resolute Kapo steps forward. 'Not the women. Men for lunch only. The women keep working.' The Kapo walks up and down, shouts the same command over and over again: 'Not the women. Men for lunch only. The women keep working.'

A few of the women approach Mosha. The Kapo watches from a distance but doesn't intervene. An older woman demands, 'What the hell, Mosha?'

She tells them, 'Leave me alone.'

A skinny woman, her ribs protruding underneath her thin linen blouse, insists, 'Just play.'

'No!' Just one word. Mosha won't explain herself to these women.

But they are angry. The older woman, who seems to be the leader of this small, incensed group from a different barrack, stands directly in front of her. 'We've lost our food and blankets because of you. And now we're out here in this heat with no water too.'

Mosha turns to walk away, but one of the women grabs her arm, tugs her back into the circle of women that has surrounded her. The woman demands, 'Fix this. We want them back.'

Mosha tells them, 'I can't.'

The skinny woman sneers, 'Or you won't.'

Mosha shrugs her arm out of the woman's grip. She walks away, a lonely figure in a place where solidarity is the only slim chance of survival.

20

It's early evening as the women file back into the camp. They are utterly exhausted. Many barely have the strength to walk; they lean on each other for support. As they walk through the gate, another Kapo waits with grim news: 'You are to go to your barrack. No food. Into the barracks. No food.'

The disgruntled women shuffle off to their barracks, barely able to put one foot in front of the other. The only noise is the rumbling of their empty stomachs. Mosha walks at the back of the line, wisely keeping her distance from everyone.

As the women enter their barracks, resigned to an evening of hunger, Josef is finishing his sumptuous meal of German sausage stew with potatoes in his quarters. Sitting at his desk, he pushes the plate to one side and picks up a stack of papers.

He knows these are important and need to be addressed, but what he really wants to do is just relax and listen to some Beethoven. He puts on one of his gramophone records, pours himself a drink and relaxes.

As Beethoven's Fifth Symphony swirls around Josef's head, it's also stuck in Mosha's brain. She runs through the notes silently in her head, eyes closed, her hands moving along to the beat, faster and faster, as though she's performing with the orchestra.

She's so engrossed in her pretend playing that she shuts out everything else around her. She doesn't see the angry looks thrown her way or the rude comments tossed in her direction. She's in a world of her own. The world of music and Beethoven. It's where she feels safe. And free.

As Mosha shuts herself off from the world, Celina is trying to make friends and smooth things over with the other women. She's sat in the middle of a group, apologising profusely: 'I'm so sorry, I didn't mean for this to happen.'

A few of the women nod sympathetically, but most are still outright hostile and upset at losing what little food they get.

One woman tells Celina, 'Everyone is fed up with your sister. She creates too much drama.'

Another adds, 'She's so much trouble.'

A third says, 'She only ever thinks of herself.'

Celina retorts, 'That sounds like Mosha!' She guesses her quip hasn't gone down that well. 'Okay, okay, I'll talk to her.'

But before she can get up, Irena stops her. 'No, I'll do it.'

They all look over to Mosha's bunk. There's a chorus of, 'Good luck,' as Irena makes her way over there. There's a rough tap on Mosha's shoulder. She opens her eyes. Irena stands over her. 'We need to talk.'

'There's nothing to say.'

'Yes, there is. If you want to survive the night in here.'

'Go on, then.'

'You need to stop thinking about yourself. It's fine if you want to defy him and refuse his presents, but don't drag us into it.'

'That wasn't my fault. I had no idea he would do that.'

'Of course it's your fault! None of this would be happening if you just played for him.'

'I've explained to you about that. I thought you understood.'

'I do. But when it begins to affect all of us, it's a whole different matter.'

'You need to stop worrying. They won't keep the food away for long. They need us to work. They can't afford for any more of us to die.'

'I wouldn't be so sure about that.'

'Just leave me alone!'

Mosha turns over on her bunk away from Irena, effectively dismissing her. Seconds later, there's another tap on her shoulder. She turns back, ready to unleash her fury on Irena, only to find Celina standing there. She scoots onto the bunk next to her sister. They hold hands in silence.

Celina speaks first. 'I'm sorry I made you mad.'

Mosha smiles at her. 'I just want you to be safe.'

'In here?'

Mosha looks up as a group of women approach them. They've had enough and not even Irena can keep them in line now.

Mosha reluctantly stands, already on the defensive, 'Don't—'

One woman, who looks ready to faint, holds up her hand to silence her. She says what everyone in the barrack is thinking: 'What's wrong with you? Just play for the man.'

But Mosha is resolute. 'I won't.'

Another woman pushes through the group. 'It's just music.'

This statement enrages Mosha. These women will never understand the power of music! She takes a few seconds to compose herself before answering, 'It's so much more than that.'

Irena steps forward. She knows how stubborn Mosha is, but also feels how desperate everyone else is. She gently says, 'Mosha. You can't do this.'

Defiant to the end, Mosha won't give an inch. 'I can do whatever I want.'

'It's not just about you anymore.'

'If it wasn't me, he'd find some other excuse.'

Irena takes Mosha's hand. 'You don't know that.'

Celina steps in. 'Look around you. Every day more and more of us die for no reason. And that's not her fault.'

Irena counters, 'But this refusal is just making it worse.'

Mosha makes one last attempt to explain. 'It's the only way I know to keep a part of me.'

The skinny woman demands to know, 'What do you mean?'

Mosha is close to tears, so Celina speaks again. 'By defying them, she stays true to herself.'

The skinny woman shrugs. 'I don't get it.'

Mosha looks each woman in the eye. 'If you die, don't you want to die as yourself? Proud and Jewish?'

The women all nod.

'And do you really think you'll do that if you bow down to them?'

A couple of the women look perplexed, but one says, 'We don't have any choice.'

'But we do. I'm not just a number on a badge. And I am proud to be Jewish. Why should I share something I love with someone I loathe?'

The skinny woman protests, 'Because we are starving to death!'

Mosha then says the words they all know are true, but no one wants to say out loud: 'We are all going to die in here anyway.' When no one says anything, she carries on. 'Who cares if it's tomorrow or six months from now?'

A now angry Irena says, 'We care. And you should too.'

Everyone's anger that's been bubbling under the surface since they arrived at the camp spills out. A fight breaks out as women start to shove each other. Once the anger has been released, there's no putting it back in the bottle – or directing it towards the real monsters who are the source of it. Instead, the women lash out at whoever is in front of them. Mosha is on the receiving end of most of the shoves and slaps. But the women are so weak and worn down, she's not in any real danger of being hurt.

Celina tries to break up the fight but it's chaos. 'Stop it!' she yells. No one is listening, so Celina climbs up onto the nearest bunk. 'Stop! Stop!' The noise quietens down. Celina carries on. 'This is what they want. They want us to turn on each other, but we need to stand together.'

Mosha adds, 'They will give us back the food.'

No one believes her. The skinny woman asks, 'Why would they?'

Mosha tries to explain. 'They need us in the fields and the factory. If we don't work, who will?'

The woman simply says, 'They'll just replace us.'

But Mosha is insistent. 'They can't replace all of us. There are too many.'

Irena rubs her face, which is slightly pink from a slap. 'Nonsense. There are more and more of us arriving every day. We're just numbers to them.'

'That's why we need to remind them we are more than just a number.' A couple of women start to nod, which encourages Mosha. 'We're all facing death in here no matter what we do, so why die following their rules?'

An older woman, who has been in this hellhole longer than any of them, tells her, 'That kind of talk will get you killed.'

But Mosha's convinced she can get them to finally listen. 'If we're going to die, we should at least do it with dignity. They can starve me and beat me, but they'll never take away my identity.'

Several of the women now nod while just a couple grumble, 'We just want our food back.'

Celina presses home Mosha's point. 'Do you really think any of us are going to walk out of this camp alive? Face facts, we're never going to leave here. So let's live by our rules, not theirs.'

The older woman says, 'None of us will be alive to have any rules if we don't get some food.'

Celina gets off the bunk, walks towards the skinny woman. Mosha grabs her arm. Stops her, shakes her head, calls out instead, 'Lotte? Where's Lotte?' The young girl pushes through the women until she's standing directly in front of Mosha.

Mosha takes her hand and tells her, 'I won't play, but I am a teacher. So, I will teach you music. The joy of music. And anyone else who wants to learn.'

Lotte squeals with delight, then remembers where she is and claps a hand over her mouth. A few of the women can't help but grin at her joy. Lotte leans in and hugs Mosha, who awkwardly hugs her back, as she cries, 'Thank you, thank you, thank you!'

Mosha smiles as she extracts herself from Lotte's embrace. She faces all the women to tell them, 'Music will be our food. We shall feed ourselves with songs and joy.'

A couple of the women clap, but more grumble and shake their heads as they walk away, still angry. The skinny woman says, 'Hmph, you can't eat music!' Irena stands nearby, watches silently, then gestures for the few women left to quieten down. Irena is still in charge here. Mosha smiles gratefully at her.

She thinks for a few seconds, trying to decide how to start her first lesson and what song to pick. 'This song is banned, but we should know it.'

Mosha starts the first verse of 'The Striped Ones'. Originally a female prisoner song written in Pawiak Prison in Warsaw, it's made its way to Majdanek, and over the next few months it will become the women's anthem.

Mosha's voice is crisp and clear and has a sweetness to it as she sings:

Their clothes veil the pride that now slumbers inside,
The boats on their feet murmur sighs,
They're brothers and sisters, they're husbands and
    wives,

The striped ones, the prisoners marked with stripes.
They're brothers and sisters, they're husbands and
     wives,
The striped ones, the prisoners marked with stripes.

Irena goes to stand next to her and joins in. Together they
sing:

The watch towers and sentinels, the barbed wire and
     gates
That cut off the world from their sight,
Cannot quell the hope that so patiently waits
For freedom to find its way inside.
Cannot quell the hope that so patiently waits
For freedom to find its way inside.

Several of the older women also join in:

This time is the time when the day lives in night,
When fate's hand knows no tender plight,
Let nothing divide us, let all here unite,
For we are the women marked with stripes.
Let nothing divide us, let all here unite,
For we are the women marked with stripes.

Some of the women are painfully out of tune, but they don't
care. For the first time since they arrived in this hell-on-earth
camp they feel a sense of camaraderie. The women who don't
know the words clap their hands or tap their feet – together.
     They carry on singing:

Let nothing divide us, let all here unite,
For we are the women marked with stripes.

Let nothing divide us, let all here unite,
For we are the women marked with stripes.

As the song ends, Irena looks questioningly at Mosha. 'And how did you learn that song?'

Mosha smiles. 'I heard one of the female political prisoners singing it one day in the yard during lunch. I asked her to sing it to me. I only have to hear a bar of music or lyrics once and I remember them.'

Irena smirks. 'Oh really?'

Mosha cheekily replies, 'It's one of my many gifts!' The women all burst out laughing. Mosha then adds, 'Actually, it's also years of practice.' The women laugh even harder. They need this bonding. They just don't realise how much.

Irena reaches under her bunk and pulls out a piece of paper and a small, stubby pencil. She writes at the top of the page: *CHOIR*.

She writes her name and then Lotte's underneath as she says, 'Anyone who wants to join the choir, write your names down here.'

About thirty women good-naturedly push and shove each other to get to the paper and add their names.

21

The men huddle around together in the bathhouse. This is one of the few times the men from all twenty-two barracks in Field I are together in the same place.

Like all the prisoners, they only get to bathe once a month – if they're lucky. They all cram into the space at once, thousands of dirty, worn-out men. They wish they had the energy to fight for what little water is made available in the poor excuse for a shower. The bigger and stronger men are usually the ones who manage a few seconds under the water, trying to wash off the dirt and get rid of the fleas. The smaller, weaker men just stand out of the way, trying to catch the splashes. They know it's pointless trying to push through. Even those who feel the luxury of water on their skin for a few precious seconds never get really clean anyway.

The guards don't bother monitoring them while they shower. It's far too cramped already in the shower room, and there are no windows they can escape from. The only way in and out is through the door, and the SS soldiers stand just outside of it, having a smoke.

This gives the men a brief chance to say their prayers and even to try to make a confession or the Eucharist. However, this is usually impossible because of the short amount of time. Holy Communion, confessions and priests are scarce in Majdanek.

The few priests that are incarcerated here prefer to take confession out in the field, or on the march back and forth each day. That way, they can at least hear what thoughts the prisoners want to unload in a semi-private setting. In the bathhouse, there are too many eyes and ears.

The only time the priests have managed to hold a Holy Communion was when a local priest in Lublin managed to get 86,000 units of consecrated bread smuggled into the camp. Once inside, Father Witold Kiedrowski, who worked in the infirmary, tried to give Communion to as many prisoners as possible. But it was so dangerous, it was never attempted again.

Still, the men look forward to the monthly showers as not only a time to cleanse their bodies but also their souls. But today, the prisoners have something else on their minds – a different but equally important agenda.

Otto Schepps steps forward, shivering in his nakedness. His ribcage can be clearly seen, while the rest of his bones protrude at all angles. He has an incessant cough – but then so do most of the men in his barrack.

Someone begins to sing the church hymn 'O *Haupt voll Blut und Wunden*' (literally, 'Oh Head, Full of Blood and Wounds', but the actual title of the hymn in English is 'O Sacred Head, Now Wounded') to provide cover. A few other voices join in but the guards outside can't really hear anything anyway.

Otto speaks up: 'So, we've all heard what has happened in the women's camp. They are being punished and starved.'

The men nod and murmur in agreement, but Ezra, one of the newer, healthier men who has only been in the camp a few days, says, 'They brought it on themselves. That Mosha woman defied the Commandant. I've only just arrived but even I know she did something that upset him.'

Otto agrees, 'Yes, she did. But now all the women are being punished. They need food, and we can give it to them.'

Ezra says, 'But it's not our problem, so why should we put ourselves in danger like that?'

Karl Baruch, who has been at the camp since it opened, steps up. He's skinnier than anyone here but also tougher. He's had to be. He tells Ezra and all the other men, 'This is the right thing to do. These are our wives, sisters, daughters, mothers. We have to help them.'

Several men agree, 'Yes!'

But Ezra won't let it go. 'Would they risk their lives for ours? Would they share their food with us?'

Otto speaks up. 'I know my wife would. And so would all of the other men's wives.'

Ezra asks, 'What about those of us that don't have wives. Or girlfriends or other family members here? We don't have anybody to look out for us.'

An angry Otto retorts, 'Of course you do. We look out for each other. That's how we survive in here.'

'Oh right, it's us against them.'

Otto might be three inches shorter and thirty pounds lighter than Ezra but he squares up for a fight. Karl quickly steps between the two men.

Karl suggests, 'Let's take a vote. Who will share their food?'

Most of the men raise their hands. A few are resistant, who, like Ezra, are new prisoners that have only been here a few days. They haven't yet had a beating or realised how much just one mouthful of bread means.

The other men throw them looks, and comments fly around the room:

'What's wrong with you?'

'That's heartless.'

'We're all in this together.'

Ezra replies, 'You can't make us give up our food.'

Karl admits, 'No, we can't. Look, most of the men want to do this, so let's agree: the men that want to give over some of their food can, and we'll make sure it's passed on. If you don't want to do it, that's fine too.'

Otto adds, 'That's fair. Let's work out how to do this.'

Most of the men nod in agreement. Ezra and the ones that don't want help move to another part of the shower room, go back to scrubbing themselves. Otto, Karl and the other men huddle together and form a plan to get as much bread as they can to the women. They only have a couple of minutes before one of the guards flings open the door and yells, 'Time.'

The men grab their grimy towels and start filing out. Ezra hangs back, making sure he's the last one out of the bathhouse. As he reaches the door, he stops, waits for the SS guard to notice he's still there.

Almost immediately, the guard realises he's not leaving. He pulls out his baton, ready to beat him, but Ezra steps further back inside so none of the men at the back of the group can see him.

Ezra raises his hands in defence. 'Please, don't hit me. I have information.'

The guard sneers at him, 'What could you possibly know?'

Ezra smiles. 'Something your commandant will want to hear. About Mosha and the women.'

'Tell me, or I will beat you.'

Ezra leans forward and tells him, 'Well, it involves bread…'

22

August 1943

The next day, men and women work side by side in the fields about a mile away from the barracks. They're already exhausted from the pre-dawn march to work. Now close to midday, the hot summer sun beats down on their backs as they work in silence, picking up stones.

SS guards walk up and down. They barely bother to acknowledge the prisoners hauling rocks from one pile to another.

Some of these stones will be used for the base of the camp's second crematorium, but generally the guards just force the prisoners to move the stones from one pile and back again. A pointless task but one that gives the guards pleasure and authority over their Jewish subordinates.

The luckier, stronger prisoners have been sent to work in nearby Lublin's SS-owned factories or plants. The 'good ones', they need to work to produce munitions for the war effort or aeroplane and vehicle parts.

But the prisoners kept to work at the camp are being forced to build their own death traps. They have no idea the rocks they are collecting are being used to construct a second crematorium.

Many of them are dying every day anyway from malnutrition, exhaustion or dysentery. There's always another newer, stronger Jew to quickly replace them. But there's no way the Commandant wants word getting out that they're building a newer, bigger crematorium so they can dispose of them even quicker and easier.

For now, the prisoners in the field just know they are being toyed with, moving rocks back and forth, back and forth. But they don't complain. To complain is to die.

Celina, her head down, is barely conscious of the figure beside her. Until he bumps into her. She turns to complain but her eyes meet the bluest eyes she's ever seen. The man, Karl Baruch, smiles. It's a dazzling smile. Karl's teeth are rotted, his dry lips cracked and his cheekbones sunken. But to Celina it's the most gorgeous smile she's ever seen.

Celina can't help but smile back. But worry flits across her as she looks around for the guards, telling him, 'We'll be beaten if they catch us talking. Or even near each other.'

Karl whispers to her, 'Don't worry, they are at the other end of the field.'

Her own smile is now grateful and welcoming. 'I'm Celina.'

Karl now seems a little shy. 'I know who you are! I'm Karl.'

Celina looks at him quizzically. 'How?'

Karl tells her, 'We all know how the Commandant has stopped your food.' Celina just stands silent, her head down. Karl reaches out, squeezes her arm. 'Everything will be fine.'

Celina implores him, 'How can you say that?'

Karl looks at her kindly. 'Because we're all in this together.'

Now Celina looks at him scornfully. 'Are you the ones being starved and beaten?'

Karl looks sadly at her. Surely she knows. 'Every single day. For different reasons. Or for no reason at all. It's happening to us too. Everyone in the camp, man or woman, is being abused.'

A guard walks towards them. Karl moves several feet away until the guard has passed. Then he steps back closer to Celina, notices she has tears in her eyes. This time she squeezes his arm. 'I'm sorry, I should've known.'

'It's fine. No one wants to admit it or say it out loud but deep down we all know what is happening to us.'

Celina smiles at him. 'Thank you.'

Karl reaches inside his dirty, worn shirt.

He pulls out something, holds it out to her. 'For you.'

Celina looks down at his hands. Bread. Karl grabs Celina's hand, puts the bread in it. It's hard and stale, like most of the food they are given, but it's still food. Celina hesitates and tries to give it back. But Karl insists, 'Take it.'

Celina tells him, 'I can't.'

Karl presses it into her hands. 'Yes, you can. We've decided to give half our food to the women until you get yours back.'

Celina looks him in the eye, holds his gaze. 'But you don't know when that will be. That bastard could withhold our food until we've all starved to death. Besides, you need it. You need it. You need the strength to work.'

Karl simply replies, 'But you need it more.'

These gentle words affect Celina more than seeing the bread in her hand. She begins to cry. Karl shifts uncomfortably. He's not used to making women cry. 'Please don't cry. I didn't mean to upset you.'

Celina smiles through the tears. 'Thank you. You don't know how much this means to me. Or the other women.' She sniffles, wipes her nose with her sleeve.

Both Celina and Karl giggle like naughty schoolchildren about to be caught out. The laughter is freeing as Celina raises her face, looks upwards, maybe searching for a sign of heaven.

She looks around; the guard is still at the other end of the field, deep in conversation with one of his fellow tormentors. She quickly leans in, steals a kiss. It's only on his cheek, but it leaves Karl blushing like a lovestruck teenager. For just a fleeting moment they could be secret lovers meeting on the sly to share their forbidden love. But this moment is deeper than any romantic love – it's a life-altering bond.

As the guard begins his stroll back to their end of the field, Celina takes the bread and slips it into her pocket. She exchanges a smile with Karl as he walks away, back over to where the men are working. They don't need words now, they have their unspoken bond of friendship. They each resume their work, moving the rocks from one pile to the other. All of a sudden, even this backbreaking work doesn't seem so bad, not when you have a friend by your side.

Later that evening, Celina sits in the middle of the barrack, a group of women crowded around her. There's some pushing and shoving as the women all try to see what's happening. Celina holds her hand up in a gesture to quieten everyone down. As silence falls across the block, Celina reaches into her pocket, pulls out the bread. Gasps fill the room.

A voice from the crowd demands, 'Where did you get that?'

All at once, dozens of women are yelling out, accusations are flying around the room. Celina holds both hands up in the air as Irena bellows, 'Quiet!'

The noise dies down. Celina waits until she can be heard. 'One of the men gave me his bread.' She places the bread on the table. 'He said the men want to help.'

One of the older, thinner women steps forward, pulls a chunk of bread out of her sleeves. 'Me too.'

Another woman pulls a piece out of her top. 'And me. One of the men gave me this on the march back.'

Several more women come forward and put bread on the table. Soon there is a pile of bread. Some of it is squashed where the women had to hide it in shoes or under their arms to get it past the guards, and most of it is stale, but to these starving women it looks like a five-course banquet.

Mosha pushes through the crowd. 'What's going on?'

An excited Celina turns to her. 'Look!'

Mosha asks, 'What is it?'

'Bread!' Mosha raises her eyebrow at her sister. Celina explains, 'It's from the men. It's their bread.'

Mosha looks stunned. 'How?' is the only word she can get out.

Celina grins at her. 'They heard what happened. They're sharing their rations with us.'

But Mosha is adamant, 'We can't take their food!'

Several dirty stares are thrown her way as Celina tells her, 'Too late.'

'But…'

Celina grabs a piece of bread from the top of the pile and shoves it into her sister's hand. 'Just stop overthinking it and eat.'

Mosha looks uncertain but Celina is already dividing up the bread between the women. There's only enough for one or two mouthfuls each but they savour each bite. It's been three days since they've had any food, and while this isn't enough to sustain them, it will stave off the hunger pains for a few more hours.

The barrack falls silent for several seconds except for the sound of chewing, which has an almost musical quality to it.

One woman declares, 'It tastes divine.'

Another adds, 'I've never had anything taste so good!'

Someone yells out, 'Mmmmmmm, all it needs is some cheese.'

'Or caviar,' shouts another.

They all laugh as Irena jokes, 'You've never had caviar in your life!'

The woman replies, 'But I can close my eyes and dream.' More laughter.

This bread has done more than just quell their hunger pains. It's given them hope. They know they are not alone. Their men – husbands, sons, brothers, uncles, nephews – who they are not supposed to have any contact with, even in the fields or around the camp, have risked their own lives to help them. It's a knowledge that fills them up when the bread doesn't.

Mosha, on her bunk, turns her piece of bread over and over in her hands. Irena appears, sits next to her. 'You have to fix this.'

Mosha sullenly replies, 'I can't stop the men giving up their food.'

An exasperated Irena tells her, 'That's not what I meant and you know it.'

Mosha opens her mouth, stops.

'No one will think any less of you.'

105

Mosha retorts, 'I don't care what the others think.'

Irena shakes her head. 'That's your problem. Please, think about them for a change.'

Mosha looks up as Celina joins them, sits at the end of the bunk. 'She's right.'

Mosha can't believe what she's hearing. 'Yesterday you were agreeing with me.'

Celina tells her, 'And today I'm not.'

Mosha opens her mouth to protest but Irena quickly pops a piece of bread in it. Mosha looks annoyed but begins to chew as Celina explains. 'What the men did, it made me realise, we're all in this together. We have to be as one.'

Mosha continues to chew the bread but has trouble swallowing it. It sticks in her throat but she forces it down. The next words from Celina are even tougher to swallow. 'All our lives I've always done everything you wanted.'

Stunned, Mosha mumbles, 'I didn't—'

But Celina presses on. 'I'm not complaining. It was how it was. I accepted that. But now I'm asking you to do this one thing for me.'

'You're asking me to go against everything I believe.'

'I know and I'm sorry. But I know you, Mosha, better than you know yourself. And I know deep down you want to help these women. I know you want to do the right thing.'

Mosha looks at Celina and Irena, the hope and expectation on their faces finally wears her down. She casts her eyes around the room, the sight of so many women with joy on their faces from a simple piece of bread. Mosha watches the women. The camaraderie they share from the experience of eating. The smiles on their faces despite the hardships they are suffering.

'I'll do it.'

Celina squeals with delight, grabs her in a huge bear hug.

23

Late August 1943

Roll call. The women stand in the early morning sun. It's 7 a.m. Roll call has been counted twice so far. Everyone is accounted for, but for some reason they haven't been released for work yet.

Then a commotion at the gates leading into Field V.

Karl and several men are being marched to the head of the compound by guards. They are pushed in front of the platform and then forced onto their knees. Several openly cry but Karl looks straight ahead, defiant.

In full uniform, Josef strolls across the compound, slowly, leisurely. He saunters past the women to join Elsa on the platform. He gives her a dazzling smile before taking the bullhorn from her. Elsa smiles back, enraptured and completely oblivious to the men awaiting their deaths right next to her.

Josef scans the women in the field. He instantly sees Mosha, fixes his stare on her. She defiantly glares back at him. He moves his gaze to Celina, who is tearful as she recognises Karl.

Josef gestures to the men kneeling below him. 'These men are being executed because they gave you their bread. Their death is on your hands.' All the women except Mosha turn their heads to the side. They cannot bear to watch what will happen next. But Mosha's eyes are locked on Josef. Their battle of wills is on show for all to see.

Elsa keeps her eyes trained on Josef. She wants to know why he's so obsessed with this goddamn Jewish whore. But he ignores her completely, only acknowledging her when he hands the bullhorn back to her.

He keeps eye contact with Mosha as he nods at the soldiers, who run and stand behind the men.

Josef nods again. The soldiers fire. BANG. BANG. BANG. The men collapse forward on the ground. Several women faint.

Elsa barks her orders. 'Get them up.'

The soldiers run among the women, haul the fallen ones to their feet, slap them back to consciousness if necessary. Tears stream down Celina's face but Mosha remains stoic as Josef turns, walks out of the compound as soldiers drag the men's bodies away.

Elsa waits until all the women are back on their feet then tells them, 'You will not defy us. You will follow orders. This is what happens when you are defiant. You are punished for a reason. How will you ever learn if you resist? It is for your own good.'

She stands on the platform just watching and waiting, taking a perverse pleasure in their misery and despair. The minutes tick by but Elsa just waits. All of a sudden the loudspeakers begin to blare out 'Nimrod' from Elgar's Enigma Variations, a classical piece usually played in remembrance to the fallen, hand-picked by Josef, and which only Mosha realises is being played as a cruel joke.

24

September 1943

Several days later and Mosha is still waiting to be called back to Josef. She's on edge. Every day that there's no word she fears the worst. While the women are still having their measly lunch and dinner withheld, they are allowed breakfast. Their punishment still stands but they need some sustenance to get them through the day. They don't realise it but if a new batch of healthier, stronger prisoners walked through the gates today, they wouldn't even get their morning coffee. They would be completely starved to death. Lucky for them, there are no new prisoners expected for at least a week.

Then, finally one day in mid-September something happens that no one was expecting.

The women are lined up for roll call. The guard on duty goes through the monotonous motion of calling out everyone's name. Today it seems like it's being rushed, and it's over within twenty minutes.

The women look around at each other, confused – until Elsa appears, hurrying across the field. A murmur runs through the women, which stops abruptly as Elsa ascends the platform.

'Today you will not be working.'

The women are stunned. Then frightened. They fear what is coming next. There have been rumours swirling around the camp for days that there have been orders to execute everyone in the camp. No one knows where these rumours started, but every prisoner has had them whispered in their ear at breakfast, in the fields and in the factories. Mosha fears Josef has finally snapped and ordered them to be killed. All because of her.

Now they all wait with bated breath to hear the order they all fear.

'Today we are moving.'

The women exchange puzzled looks as Elsa continues, 'The women's camp is being moved from Field V to Field I. You will move to the barracks there and this camp will become the infirmary. You will gather all your belongings. Your clothing, blankets and your mattress, if you have one. You will all make sure your barrack is completely spotless and clean. Any barrack that does not pass inspection will result in punishment. You have two hours to be ready to move to the new camp.'

The women stand rooted to the spot, completely surprised by the news.

Elsa screams at them, 'Go!'

The women all run in different directions to their barracks. They all grab their possessions and drag them outside and lay them carefully on the ground. Then for the next two hours they scrub and clean, knowing if they leave even one inch of the hut not up to Elsa's standards, they are in for yet another beating.

The guards have supplied rags and just one bucket of dirty water per barrack, but the women are determined to make everything shine. Mosha and several other women wipe down the bunks while others are on their knees scrubbing the floor.

Lice scurry out of the way or crawl over the women as they try their hardest to make the hut look presentable.

Maria mutters, 'They're going to need to disinfect this place before they use it as a hospital.'

Helena says, 'They should've disinfected it months ago. I know that's why we feel sick so often.'

The women all murmur their agreement as they keep buffing the same spots over and over again to make sure it will meet Elsa's approval.

At the two-hour mark, a guard appears at the door and yells, 'Roll call.'

Maria exclaims, 'Not again!' There are groans as the women head outside and reluctantly line up. But this time the count is quick and the women are instructed to grab all their belongings.

Elsa informs them: 'You will follow the guard barrack by barrack. Barrack 1 will leave first, then 2 and so on.

When you arrive in Field I, you will line up for roll call again.'

The women groan inwardly but dare not complain out loud. They set off, leaving behind Field V. Normally it should only take twenty minutes to walk between the two fields, but today's march takes close to an hour.

The women shuffle along as they struggle to carry the mattresses, blankets and clothing. They work in teams of three, with each trio responsible for whatever was connected to their bunk. All of them have put on as much clothing as they can as two of the women from the trio carry the mattress between them while the third carries the blankets and any clothes they can't wear.

The walk is slow and laborious, with mattresses being dropped every few yards. The first time one is dropped the women quiver, waiting for the inevitable beating, but surprisingly it doesn't come. The soldiers just yell, 'Pick it up, keep moving.'

They finally all reach Field I and are surprised to find it's almost an identical replica to Field V – except there are two extra barracks.

A guard now yells, 'Roll call,' as the women form their lines and wait to be counted for the fifth time today. When the count is over, Elsa reappears.

'You will continue to live in the same corresponding barracks. If you were in Barrack 1 before, you are in 1 now, 2 for 2 and so on. You will need to clean your new homes before you move your belongings inside. Again, you have two hours. Dismissed.'

The women walk – not run – over to their new homes. Mosha finds herself next to Irena. 'Did the men not clean them like we cleaned ours? What state are they in?'

'I'm sure the men were forced to clean too. This is just out of spite, something for us to do because we're not in the fields working. They can't let us have just one afternoon off when we could be doing manual labour!'

Irena's theory proves to be right – the barrack appears spotless, cleaned to within an inch of its life. But waiting just inside the door are the rags and water – the same filthy water the men used earlier. The women once again leave their belongings outside and each grabs a rag as they pass through the door.

This time, guards stand at the door along with a Block Elder and watch as they re-clean everything the men have already done. The women choose the bunks they want and then get to cleaning them and the area around them. Mosha is wiping down one of the lower bunkbeds when she notices it's swarming with both fleas and lice. She jumps back out of the way, almost knocking over Maria.

'Hey, watch it!'

'This bunk is infected with fleas and lice.'

'You should be used to them by now!'

'This is worse than I've ever seen.'

Mosha walks over to the Block Elder; she doesn't wait for her to address her and instead asks, 'Can we please get some disinfectant?'

'Why?'

'This place is infested with fleas and lice. We need disinfectant to make it clean.'

'You're lying, there are no fleas in here.'

'Please. Look, I already have flea bites.' Mosha holds out her hand. The Block Elder peers at it but tells her, 'No.'

Mosha doesn't want a beating but she also doesn't want to catch typhoid either. 'Please. *Oberaufseherin* Klein said we had to clean the barracks until they were spotless. We can't do that if there are all these bugs. Can you just ask?'

The mention of Elsa strikes the fear of God into the Block Elder. She doesn't need a reprimand from Klein, which is just another way of saying a whipping, but she also doesn't want to get into trouble for the barrack being unclean. Which is the lesser of two evils?

'Alright,' she resignedly agrees and disappears into the field. Mosha goes back over to the bunk and pretends to wipe it down. Right now she has no intention of putting her precious hands anywhere near any fleas or lice.

A short time later the Block Elder reappears – and the look on her face says it all. She shakes her head at Mosha. 'There is no disinfectant available. Besides, Klein believes if you scrub hard enough, you will get this barrack completely clean.'

Mosha is fuming inside but there's nothing she can do about it. She goes back over to her bunk, takes off her shoe and starts pummelling anything within a three-foot radius of the bunk. All the other women stop to watch her.

Maria sees what she is doing and joins her. The two of them look like they are beating the hell out of their own bed. Matylda wanders over and asks, 'What are you doing?'

With each whack Mosha replies, 'Killing. Every. Last. One. Of. These. Damn. Bugs.'

Soon every woman has one shoe off and they begin banging away in harmony. There's an almost musical quality to the beat. They get into a rhythm and several women, including Mosha and Lotte, begin humming along.

Soon, without realising it, they are singing, and not a sanctioned German song but a clandestine song titled 'O Majdanek Our Life and Death' – a song that has recently been written by one of the male prisoners and passed throughout the camp.

The women sing together:

There never has been,
Nor will there ever be,
Anywhere on earth,
A sun like that which shines
Upon our Majdanek.

They are so intent on the task at hand that they don't hear
Elsa enter the barrack. Slowly the singing falters as one by
one the women realise she's standing there, until only Mosha
and Maria, who are still heartily banging away with their
shoes, are still singing.

Maria notices Elsa first and abruptly stops and quickly
elbows Mosha. Mosha looks at Maria, and out of the corner
of her eye sees Elsa. She stands up straight and turns to
face her.

Elsa is trying to keep her temper in check. 'What do you
think you are doing?'

Mosha knows she's going to be punished no matter what,
so she flippantly replies, 'Cleaning.'

'That's not what I meant.'

'I was just following orders, trying to get rid of the lice –
without any disinfectant.'

The women stand there, mouths open, aghast at Mosha
answering back to *Oberaufseherin* Klein.

They are more afraid for her than she is for herself.

Elsa steps closer to her. 'I meant the singing.'

Offhandedly, Mosha replies, 'Oh that? I thought we were
allowed to sing while working. The guards always make us
sing in the fields. And isn't this work?'

Elsa is incensed. She knows technically Mosha is right,
yet every inch of her is itching to slap the reasoning out of

her. 'It was the song you were singing. It's not an authorised German song.'

Mosha, acting all innocent now, tells her, 'I thought it was a sanctioned camp song.' She adds sweetly, 'It's just about how great life is here in Majdanek.'

This tips Elsa over the edge. 'You will not sing that song ever again. If you do, you will be sent to the gas chamber.'

Silence. Elsa realises what she has said, the threat she has made. Everyone knows what happens to prisoners when they are taken away and never come back, but this is the first time it's been openly acknowledged in the camp.

Elsa can feel all eyes on her, but tells herself she's in charge, she doesn't have to explain herself to anyone in this room. She leans in close so her face is just inches away from Mosha's. 'This is your last warning.'

25

The following evening, Mosha sits on her new bunk as several women, including Lotte, sit at her feet, an enraptured audience waiting for their next lesson. Mosha taps a wooden fork on her bunk while the women warm up their voices.

When the women finish their scales, Mosha leans in to tell them, 'Now remember, this song is "Arbeit Macht Frei". It's about how work will set you free. So, don't sing it in the fields if they ask you for a song. It's been banned.'

A worried Lotte asks, 'Should we learn this then?'

An older woman scoffs, 'Of course we should.'

But Mosha warns her, 'Yes. But just don't sing it in front of a guard.'

Lotte nods. 'Do you think we'll ever sing outside the camp?'

Mosha and the older woman exchange a knowing glance. But she doesn't want to crush the young girl's dreams. 'Maybe. One day.'

Lotte gets a dreamy look in her eyes. 'Can you see us on the stage? The lights. The audience. The music!'

Mosha laughs. 'That's some dream.'

But there's no stopping Lotte now as she gushes, 'Do you really think it could happen? Do you? Will I ever share a stage with you? That would be so incredible!'

Mosha tells her, 'Only if you learn the songs.'

But now the dream is getting bigger and bigger. 'Will you teach me to play the piano too?'

'One day.'

Mosha taps the fork again to signal the conversation is over. Lotte settles in to listen as Mosha sings the lyrics slowly so the other women can learn:

Barbed wire, loaded with death
Is drawn around our world.
Above a sky without mercy
Sends frost and sunburn.
Far from us are all joys.

Lotte is about to cry. She wipes away a single tear that has rolled down her cheek. 'It's a really sad song. I want to sing something happy. Why can't we sing 'Ahava'?'

Irena tuts, 'You silly girl. We are learning these songs because the *Lagerführer* doesn't want us to.'

Lotte nods and sniffles at the same time. Mosha leans over and gives her shoulder a little squeeze.

'It's good that you feel that way. Songs are supposed to make you feel sad. Or happy. Or joyful. Or even angry. Lean into it. Feel the emotion.'

Mosha taps the fork, the women sing in unison. Even though they sing quietly, barely above a whisper so they don't attract the attention of the guards, they sound beautiful. United.

They sing together:

Barbed wire, loaded with death
Is drawn around our world.
Commotion at the door.

As they sing the last line, a woman cries out, 'Guard!' With their own commotion at the door, the women scatter as Elsa strides through the barrack. She walks around, randomly picking up blankets and throwing them on the floor. The women just keep their eyes cast downwards; no one wants to incur her wrath.

One woman dares to look up just as Elsa is passing. Elsa stops, pulls her SS-issued dagger from the scabbard hanging at her waist. Etched on the blade is the SS motto, *Meine ehre heisst treue* (My honour is loyalty). The blade cuts through the woman's meagre blanket. It rips the threadbare blanket to shreds. And slices into the woman's knee. Blood seeps through what little fabric remains draped over the woman's legs. She tries not to cry out, but a whimper escapes her lips.

Elsa grabs the woman by the chin, forces her to look into her eyes as she plunges the knife into her leg. The woman screams out in pain. Elsa triumphantly looks around the barracks. Everyone stares at the floor. She twists the knife.

The screams get louder. Elsa pulls the knife out. Blood drips from the blade onto the floor. She leans over, wipes the blade on someone else's blanket lying nearby.

Elsa reveals, 'She stole from the *Führer*. She took something that didn't belong to her from the warehouse.'

Elsa reaches under the woman's mattress on her bunk and pulls out a small baby rattle. It's not expensive. It's not made of silver. It's just a plain wooden rattle. The sight of it makes the woman cry out, 'It is mine. It's my son's.'

Elsa snatches it out of her reach. 'No. Everything in the warehouse belongs to the *Führer*. You have no belongings here. You deserve no belongings here.'

She steps away from the woman just as she faints and slumps to the floor. Before Elsa can even step over her, two guards rush over and drag the woman out of the barrack. The silence is deafening but the atmosphere is heavy with hate.

Mosha stands up but Celina yanks her back onto the bunk. Elsa turns at the noise. She's can't see Mosha and Celina's bunk but she just knows it's her. She strides down the aisle. Women scrabble out of her way. No one else wants to be in the line of fire.

Elsa stops in front of Mosha, who refuses to look at her. She pokes her in the shoulder with the tip of her knife. It's not hard enough to draw blood but strong enough to make Mosha flinch. Begrudgingly, Elsa finally reveals another reason why she's there: 'The Commandant wants to see you.'

Mosha tries to sound surprised. 'Me? Why?'

Elsa is itching to stick the knife in her neck but she's under strict orders to deliver Mosha – unharmed – to Josef's hut. She simply says in her sternest voice, 'You don't get to ask questions.' She then grabs Mosha's arm, yanks her upright into a standing position.

Mosha looks over at Celina and Irena, gives them a little nod. They nod back. They know the plight she's facing by going to Josef's hut. They each make a silent prayer that she'll be able to go through with it.

Elsa roughly shoves Mosha in front of her, gives little pushes all the way out of the barrack.

26

Elsa marches Mosha across the compound, towards Josef's hut. Mosha stumbles a couple of times but manages not to fall. She's exhausted and hungry but she won't give Elsa the satisfaction of kicking her while she's down.

As they near the hut, Elsa draws Mosha near, leans in. 'I have no idea why he's obsessed with a pathetic little Jew like you. Do not encourage him.' Mosha wisely stays quiet as Elsa points to her badge. 'Remember, you are nothing here.'

They reach the door of Josef's hut. Elsa knocks, waits for Josef to open the door. She pushes Mosha inside, then starts to take a step into the hut herself. But Josef blocks her and tells her, 'Thank you,' before shutting the door in her face.

Elsa is so stunned – and furious – she stands on the outside of the door for a few seconds, unsure what to do. But there is nothing for her to do but stalk back across the compound.

Inside the hut, Mosha stands by the door. She can't bring herself to make the first move. Just being near him makes her skin crawl. She closes her eyes. In her head she hears the opening refrain to Beethoven's *Fidelio*. The story of personal sacrifice, heroism and eventual triumph, with its underlying struggle for liberty and justice, calms her down.

Josef walks over to the table, picks up a glass of wine, gulps it down, then slowly turns to face Mosha. 'Are you ready to play now?'

Mosha opens her eyes but still hesitates, allowing Josef's narcissism to rear its ugly head. 'I know everything.' When Mosha doesn't reply, he continues. 'I knew the men were going to give you their food before they even did it.'

Stunned, Mosha replies, 'You knew?'

Josef sneers, 'Of course I knew. This is my camp. I know everything that happens here.'

'But you didn't stop them!'

'I let it happen. Production cannot fall. We are on a schedule. This way, you got some food, someone still gets punished for breaking the rules, but production doesn't drop.'

Mosha knows she shouldn't argue with him but she just can't help herself. 'That's all you care about. We are nothing but irritating numbers to you.'

Josef walks over, stops directly in front of Mosha, reaches out, touches her hair. She tries not to flinch, but he sees the struggle. His caress travels from her hair down her cheek to her neck. His hand stops just below her chin. All he has to do is squeeze.

He quickly removes his hand. 'You know that's not true. Not for you.'

Mosha looks up, their eyes lock. 'I don't want…' Even without his hand around her neck Mosha chokes and can't get the words out.

Josef asks in a hushed tone, 'What do you want?'

They stand barely an inch apart but neither moves. Mosha finds her voice. 'I want you to give the women their food back. You can starve me but please don't punish them. It's not their fault.'

'The women can have their food back any time. All you need to do is play. Just one song.' Mosha searches his eyes. Josef holds her gaze. 'There must be something you want.'

'I just told you—'

Josef cuts her off. 'You told me what the women want. What do you want?'

Mosha admits, 'I can't tell you.' It's like someone flicked a switch and the loving, caring Josef is now standing in front of her.

'I'm the only one here you can tell.'

Mosha breaks eye contact, embarrassed, but Josef reaches out, tilts her chin until their eyes lock again. Mosha tries to wriggle out of his grasp but he holds her face firm.

'I know you want to play. With every bone in your body, you want to touch those keys. You want to be on that stage again. Sitting at the piano. The music sweeping over the crowd. The applause. That's what you really want.'

Mosha nods, tears in her eyes.

'There's no shame in that. I want it for you too.'

Mosha turns away from him, chokes back a sob, embarrassed. But more than that, she's angry at herself. Angry that she's shown weakness. 'I can't.'

Josef grabs her shoulders, 'Yes you can.' Mosha tries to break free but can't. 'One song.'

She doesn't believe him. 'Just one song? And the women get the food back? And the blankets?'

Josef leaves her hanging for a few seconds. 'Yes.'

Mosha pushes her luck. 'Extra rations.'

'What?'

'All the prisoners get extra rations at dinner.'

Josef thinks it over. 'They can have extra rations if you do one more thing.'

Mosha's curiosity gets the better of her. She knows she should refuse; agreeing will only give him ever more power over her, but she blurts out, 'What?'

Josef turns and walks into his bedroom. He's gone just moments and returns with a dusky-pink gown. It evokes in Mosha a thousand painful memories from a thousand years ago. He holds it out to her. It's the most beautiful thing she's seen in a very long time. She wants to reach out and touch it but the voice in her head tells her not to.

'I want you to wear this while you play.'

When Mosha doesn't answer him, Josef demands, 'Do you want the extra rations or not?'

He holds out the dress. She approaches. Despite the voice in her head now screaming, Mosha reaches out, touches it gently. Josef gestures to the bedroom. Mosha takes the dress as he pours a drink, downs it in one, pours another. He turns, eyes trained on the bedroom door.

Mosha appears. The dress hangs from her gaunt frame but it's transformed her into some otherworldly, ethereal creature. Josef inhales sharply. 'Beautiful.'

Mosha can't bear to look at him as the shame washes over her. She walks over to the piano, sits down. Josef stands behind her, places his hands on her shoulders, closes his eyes. He's transported back to the living room in his family's mansion, twenty-four years ago:

Josef, seventeen, stands behind his mother Greta, at the piano. She wears the same pink silk gown. His hands on her shoulders as she plays Wagner. She finishes, half turns to him, takes one of his hands, pulls him onto the stool next to her. She places one hand on his thigh, starts another tune with the other hand. He puts his head on her shoulder, her hand caresses higher, higher up his thigh as the music's tempo quickens.

27

A dozen women huddle together in the darkness. Afraid of attracting the guards' unwanted attention, they keep their voices low while one stands near the door as a lookout. Most of the women in the block pretend to be asleep or have drifted off from sheer exhaustion. Always in charge, Irena directs her question at Celina: 'You're sure she'll do it?'

Celina whispers back, 'Yes. She promised me she would.'

'How do you know she'll keep that promise?'

'I know my sister. She's stubborn as a mule, but when she makes a promise she always keeps it.'

'I hope you're right for all our sakes.'

Celina holds in her anger. 'You'll see.'

Across the compound, Mosha is struggling. She looks up at Josef, who is lost in a trance. A host of emotions flit across his face. He's not in the room with her; he's somewhere else, far, far away.

Mosha touches one of the keys; it pings, bringing Josef out of his dream. He has a sharp intake of breath at the unexpected plink. Without realising it, he whispers, '*Mutter!*'

Mosha twists around and looks at him in complete horror. She knows why he was so adamant she wear this gown while playing. 'This was your mother's dress!'

'Yes.'

Mosha tries to wriggle out of his grasp; the fabric feels like it's burning through her skin. But Josef's fingers just press down harder and harder into her shoulders. She yells, 'Get this thing off of me.'

But Josef won't release her. He finally has her exactly where he's spent hours and hours dreaming of. He wants this private concert more than life itself. 'PLAY!'

Mosha is still squirming under his grip. The realisation quickly dawns on her that she can't get free. She's trapped. The only way to end this nightmare will be to play for him. She's going to have to keep her promise. Dressed as his mother.

She reluctantly turns, faces the piano. Her fingers run up and down the keys. The familiarity hits them both hard. Josef leans back, closes his eyes as she runs her fingers up and down the keys. Mosha takes a deep breath, begins to play the first bar of Beethoven's Symphony No. 9 in D minor – 'Ode to Joy'.

But there's no joy as she plays. Her fingers fly across the ivories. She doesn't miss a note. It's technically perfect but there's no passion, no ecstasy. By the second bar, Josef realises she's just going through the motions. He steps back, stunned. For a moment he's lost, unsure what is happening. He knows the tune but it's cold, aloof. It sounds nothing like Mosha's usual arousing performance.

'Stop! Stop it. What are you doing?'

In his rage, Josef slams down the piano lid on her fingers. Mosha doesn't have time to snatch her hands out of the way. Pain shoots through her precious fingers, but luckily there's no permanent damage. Mosha jumps up from the stool, cradling her throbbing hands.

Josef takes a step towards her. She involuntarily takes a step backwards. The look on his face momentarily frightens her. Anger then puzzlement flicker across his face as he demands, 'Where is the passion? Where is the joy?'

Mosha can't believe what she's hearing. Surely he knows why? Surely he doesn't expect her to play like she's in a dazzling concert hall before the world's elite?

'How do you expect me to feel those in here?' she asks.

He responds, 'How can you not feel that passion every time you play?'

Now she's just as angry as him. 'You can't force me to feel those things! You're being ridiculous.'

Josef steps towards her, grabs her wrist. With her free hand, Mosha slaps him hard across the face. The rage in her is getting bigger by the second. She tells him, 'You wanted me to play. I played. I hate you!'

'I lo—'

'NO! Don't you dare say it.'

A petulant Josef doesn't say the words, but insists, 'But I do.'

'No, you don't. You just love the idea of owning me and the music.'

Without waiting for a reply, Mosha grabs the dress around the neckline. She tugs at it, hard. It tears across the shoulders. She tugs and tugs until she rips it off. She throws it at Josef. It lands at his feet.

Mosha stands in front of him in her threadbare underwear, but she's too incensed to care or cover up. He bends down, tenderly picks up the dress, cradles it almost like a baby. Before he can admonish her, Mosha blurts out, 'I thought you understood.'

He says softly, 'I do. I know exactly how you feel.'

'LIAR!'

Josef gently lays the dress over his desk, turns and reaches for her, but Mosha quickly steps out of his grasp.

'You're a fraud.' With each word she takes a step further away.

Josef lets her. He won't beg again. He believes he has other ways to make Mosha do what he wants. 'And you've just sealed everyone's fate.'

Mosha knows she shouldn't argue or antagonise him any further, but she just can't stay quiet. She taunts him. 'Because you can't get what you want?'

In stark contrast, Josef is calm and collected. 'Everyone who has been helping you will come to regret their decision.'

Mosha defiantly tells him, 'We're stronger than you know.'

Josef smirks. 'Don't worry, they'll get their extra rations for that pathetic little display. For now. But they will pay for your disobedience. But I think it's time to teach you a lesson, right now. On your knees.'

Mosha looks confused as Josef takes a step in her direction, his voice suddenly stern and cold. 'I said, get on your knees.' He pulls the pistol out of the holster sitting on his hip. He points it straight at her. Stunned, Mosha automatically sinks to her knees as Josef stands next to her. She instinctively shuts her eyes tight.

As Josef presses the gun against the back of her head, she immediately throws her head forward towards the floor. Josef's ruthless laughter rings out. He could end this now, but he wants his fun. He wants to play awhile, teach Mosha a lesson.

'Open your eyes.' She refuses, keeping them scrunched tight. 'Open. Your. Eyes.' With each word, he taps her on the side of the head with the nozzle of the gun.

Mosha reluctantly opens her eyes but looks straight ahead. She doesn't want to see him or the weapon. Josef shifts position and stands directly in front of her.

Oh God, no, not that, not that.

But he moves to her side and now holds the gun next to her right ear but points it away from her. He fires towards the door. BANG. The noise ricochets round and round Mosha's head but the sound leaves her reeling – and deaf.

Without any remorse, Josef tells her, 'Now let's see you hear your beloved Beethoven.'

Mosha shakes her head but it's not an answer to his question. She's desperately trying to pull herself out of the fog that has descended over her. Blood trickles out of her ear. She hasn't heard a word he's said.

Josef puts his face right next to her red and bleeding ear. 'You want to play now?'

Mosha unintentionally ignores him. She's lost in a sea of deafening silence. Josef grabs her by the shoulders, shakes her back and forth. She looks up at him in a daze.

He drags Mosha to the door, opens it, shoves her out, slams the door shut. Furious at Mosha but even more mad at himself, he throws his pistol across the room. He grabs the wine, downs it in one gulp. He walks over to his desk, picks up his mother's tattered dress, sinks into the chair, cradles the dress like a lover, rubbing his face into the torn dusky fabric.

Josef closes his eyes and is once again transported back to another time and place:

He's nine years old and sitting at the top of the grand staircase in his family's mansion. Behind him stretches a dark hallway leading back to his bedroom, where he should be tucked in and fast asleep. But he's been enticed to sneak out of his room by the party below. He peers through the ornate iron balustrades, eager to catch a glimpse of the dazzling guests milling around.

A huge decorated fifteen-foot Christmas tree stands in the middle of the foyer. Decorations adorn every inch of the house, while a six-person choir stands off to the side, angelically singing a mixture of hymns and Christmas songs.

Josef pushes his head through the banister, careful not to get stuck, but desperate to see everything that is happening. Guests are still arriving, and a butler in full evening livery greets them at the door before loudly announcing them.

Josef has watched this scene a dozen times before but it still excites him and leaves him a little awestruck. Dukes, earls, lords even a king or two are down there, just out of his reach, enjoying the festivities.

He inches forward a little more, straining as he hears his mother Greta's voice just moments before she sweeps into view. Dressed in the pink gown, she seems to float across the foyer to greet her most important guest, who has just arrived: the German Emperor, Friedrich Wilhelm Viktor Albert, also known as Wilhelm II.

Josef watches, fascinated, as the Emperor fawns over his mother, kisses her hand and then escorts her from the foyer into the grand ballroom. Once they disappear from view, Josef thinks about scooting further down the stairs but knows the trouble he'll be in if he's discovered. He's still thinking about risking it when the music wafts up the stairs from the ballroom.

Even without being able to see, he knows it's his mother playing. In his mind, he can clearly see her sitting at the piano, his favourite pink gown spread out over the stool as Greta begins to play one of Johann Strauss's most famous pieces, 'An der schönen blauen Donau' (The Beautiful Blue Danube).

The noise and chatter die down as everyone makes their way into the ballroom to fully appreciate Greta and her exquisite playing. With everyone in the ballroom, Josef decides it's safe to slowly slide further and further down the staircase until he can see into the ballroom.

A huge glittering silver eight-light Givenchy chandelier illuminates the room, giving it an ethereal glow and an almost magical feel as couples begin to waltz to Greta's playing. There are looks of pure joy on people's faces as they whirl round and round the room.

At first Josef smiles at the sight, but his own joy is quickly replaced by something he's not felt before. It grows and grows, and he becomes angry that these people are enjoying his mother's music.

How dare they? This is his mother and his music. He doesn't want to share her with anyone! Josef turns and stomps back up the stairs. He runs into his bedroom, flings himself onto his bed, pulls his pillow over his head to try and block out the faint music. He can still see his mother, but she is looking up at the Emperor, who stands next to the piano. Josef knows that look. It's the look reserved for him when he sits on her lap. Tears of frustration and anger mingle as he scrunches the pillow tighter and tighter, almost suffocating himself. He eventually sobs himself to sleep.

Josef opens his eyes, once again wet with tears of anger and frustration. He dabs at his eyes with the tattered dress, sniffs it one last time before he gets up and walks into the bedroom.

He gently and carefully lays the dress out on one side of the bed, the neckline resting just below the pillow. He lays on the other side of the bed on his back for a few seconds, before turning on his side, facing the dress. He drapes his arm over it, like a lover, closes his eyes and drifts off into a troubled sleep.

28

Mosha lands in a heap outside Josef's hut. The door slams shut behind her but she hears nothing. For a few minutes she just lies in the mud. Tears stream down her face but she refuses to call out for help. Even if she did, she wouldn't be able to hear anyone reply; all she can hear right now is an incessant ringing in both ears.

She sees two guards walking the perimeter of the fence in the distance. She pulls herself together, completely unaware there's a guard standing to the left of Josef's door. He's yelling at her back, 'You, get up, get up.' When she doesn't respond, he kicks Mosha in the back and sends her sprawling again.

As she lays face down in the dirt, he places a heavy boot on her back between her naked shoulder blades, pushes her into the wet, sticky earth. The smell of nature permeates all of Mosha's other senses. With her hearing gone, everything else suddenly feels magnified. She can taste the earth on her lips, the smell infiltrates her nose and everything looks so vibrant. The touch of the ground electrifies her, gives her the strength to rise.

She wriggles out from under the guard's boot. He lets her stand. Mosha turns to face him. She thrusts her tin badge at him, points at her number. His mouth is moving but she has no idea what he is saying. Unaware she is shouting, she tells him, 'I can't hear you.'

The guard carries on talking but Mosha just shakes her head at him, then points to her ear. She yells, 'I think I'm deaf.'

The guard doesn't believe her and pokes her with his rifle. Mosha understands this and starts walking across the compound towards her block, holding her ear, pressing on it to stop the bleeding. The guard stays by Josef's door but keeps his rifle trained on her until she reaches the gate in the fence that separates the Nazis' living accommodations from the prisoner section.

Mosha turns and looks back at Josef's hut before slipping through the gate back into another kind of hell. She approaches the door to her block but hesitates outside. She looks a mess but there's nothing she can do about that.

Her clothes are still in Josef's hut and there's no way she can wash off the mud that's caked down her arms and legs. But she rubs her tear-stained face; she doesn't want the other women to know she's been crying. She tries to even out the dirt as a sob catches in her throat. She takes a minute to compose herself before pushing open the door to the barracks.

As she walks through the hut, a hush descends over the room. Women strain to look at her but no one dares speak to her as she passes their bunks.

Exhausted, Mosha throws herself on her bunk, while Celina scrabbles to get out of the way as several women, led by Irena, rush over. Mosha turns away from everyone, faces the wall, trying to shut out their faces.

The women stand by the bunk, all firing questions at the same time:

'Did you play for him?'

'What did you play?'

'Was he pleased?'

'Are we getting our food back?'

'Where are your clothes?'

Celina gently asks, 'Did you keep your promise?' Nothing. Celina taps Mosha on the shoulder. She shrugs her off. Celina grabs her shoulder, pulls her body towards her, gasps when she sees the streaks of blood running from her ear down her neck. 'What the hell happened?'

Mosha looks at her sister, tears well in her eyes. She squeezes them shut as the tears begin to flow. 'Tell me,' Celina says softly.

Mosha simply points to her ear, then makes a gesture for a gun being fired. The women look stunned and immediately start firing questions at her again:

'What did you do?'

'Why did he do that?'

'Why did…'

Mosha looks around wildly. She feels like an animal trapped in a cage. Even though she can't hear what they are saying, the angry energy is coming off them in waves.

Celina cuts them off, 'Stop! She can't hear you.'

Irena adds, 'Give her some space.'

The women, except Celina and Irena, back off. 'We just want to know what happened,' one of them says.

Irena tells her, 'And you will. But for now, we need to fix her ear.'

Celina rips off a small piece of her skirt and tries to wipe the blood away from Mosha's ear. She says loudly, 'You need a doctor.' But Mosha just looks blankly at her. Celina leans in closely to her uninjured left ear, 'You need a doctor!'

Despite the ringing and the muffled voice, Mosha understands what she's said. Mosha shouts back, 'I'm fine. It's just a ruptured eardrum. It will fix itself. And when the ringing stops, I'll be able to hear better.'

Celina shouts into her left ear, 'You do realise you're shouting?'

At the absurdity of it all, Mosha laughs, which prompts Irena to ask, 'Why is she laughing? It's not funny.'

Mosha points at her head, closes her eyes, sways.

'What is she doing?' Irena adds.

Celina grins as she explains, 'She used to do that when we were children when she didn't want to speak or listen to anyone. It used to infuriate our mother.'

But Irena is confused. 'I still don't understand why she's laughing.'

Celina continues, 'She's imagining a concert in her head. She's in her own little world, blocking out everyone else. She hears music and applause. She chooses what she wants to hear – and I'm guessing right now she's choosing not to hear us or the Commandant yelling at her to play!'

Celina starts to laugh, then Irena, finally understanding, joins in. Lotte, across the aisle, sitting on her own bunk with six other women, chimes in, 'And she can't hear how bad your singing is now either, Irena!'

Irena laughs even harder before managing to gasp, 'Why you cheeky little…' The laughter is infectious, and soon most of the women are laughing, something they haven't done for a very long time.

Mosha senses something is happening. She opens her eyes, swings her legs around and looks at the women, all laughing together. She nudges Celina and makes a writing gesture in the air.

Celina yells, 'Pen?'

Mosha nods. Someone passes forward a stubby two-centimetre pencil and a piece of scrap brown paper. Mosha mouths, 'Thank you.' She knows how precious these items are in the camp. For someone to relinquish them without bartering means a lot. But now Mosha hesitates. She knows the woman who gave these up is expecting good news – news that she's performed for Josef and struck a bargain.

She writes quickly, hands the piece of paper to Celina. She scans it, looks at Mosha, who nods for her to read it aloud.

Celina clears her throat, which gains the attention of the women. They eagerly wait to find out what Mosha has done for them. Celina states, 'Our food is being returned. But he knew before the men helped, so that's why they were punished.'

Mosha motions to Celina to hand her back the paper. She scribbles down more words.

'What is she saying now?' The same woman sounds hostile. A murmur runs through the barrack.

Celina continues, 'The Commandant has said that there will be extra rations, but Mosha doesn't believe him. She says we need to be careful, to not put our trust in anything he says.'

Irena says, 'We need to stay as one.'

Most of the women nod in agreement, although a few look disgruntled and head back to their bunks. Irena leans over, squeezes Mosha's hands and mouths the words, 'Thank you.'

29

Late October 1943

Josef sits in his chair, flicking through a pile of requests from both the SS and the prisoners, when the phone rings.

He answers, 'Yes. This is *SS-Gruppenführer* Hanke. Good evening, sir.'

He shuffles through the stack of papers on the desk. Pulls out a sheet, looks over it before speaking into the receiver, 'Right now I have 22,354 prisoners in total. Of those, 15,421 are Jews.'

On the other end of the line is *SS-Oberst-Gruppenführer* Helldorf, fifty-nine, sitting at his desk in the Nazi HQ in Berlin. A Nazi flag on a stand flutters to his right, a painting of Adolf Hitler adorns the wall behind him. Helldorf is all business, no nonsense; he has no time for pleasantries. 'How many men, how many women?'

Josef responds, 'I have around 19,000 men and 3,000 women.'

'I have 18,000 *häftlings* that need to be moved.'

'I currently only have room for another 2,000.'

'You need to lose 18,000 to make way for the new ones.'

'Why don't you just execute those 18,000?'

'They have just joined us. They are much stronger than what you have, better to work.'

'I see.'

'How quickly can you dispose of them?'

'Crematorium 1 has been operational for a while, and we just completed the second one.

'Using the crematoriums will take too long. I need it done in one day.'

'That's tough. But if we use a firing squad—'

Helldorf cuts him off mid-sentence. 'Lose all the women and then 18,000 of the men. Make sure you dispose of all the Jews.'

'I need to keep some of the women.'

'Why? We need the men to build. There's no use for women.'

'They are entertainment for the soldiers. They are good for morale. And in the kitchen.'

Helldorf takes a second to think it over. 'Keep fifty then.'

'And I can pick which ones?'

'Yes. I'll start the march shortly.'

'When will they arrive?'

'Sometime early November, so we need to make this happen soon. The camps at Trawniki and Poniatowa are also getting the same orders. We will co-ordinate a date.'

'Yes, sir.'

'We are calling it Operation Harvest Festival.'

Both men hang up. Josef sighs, pulls out another stack of papers from a drawer. He sorts them into two piles. The top sheet on the left pile has the headline *Jews with skills*. The right pile simply says *Jews*. They are all men's names. He starts putting ticks against names on the right-hand pile.

He opens his desk drawer and pulls out a sheet of blank paper. At the top he writes: *WOMEN TO KEEP*.

The first name under the title is, of course, Mosha's. Then he writes Celina's. Crosses it out, thinks for a few seconds, and then writes it in again. Irena's name is next, but then he has no idea who any of the other women are in Mosha's barrack or in the choir.

He jumps up from the desk and yanks open the door to his house with such force, he startles the SS guard standing outside.

He hands the young lad a blank piece of paper. 'Go to where the women are working. Find either Mosha Gebert or some woman called Irena and get them to write down all the women that are in the choir.'

'Yes, sir.'

The young lad takes off at full speed as Josef heads back inside. He sits back at the desk and goes back to picking the non-Jewish men with any type of skill to keep. He doesn't save any male Jews at all.

As Josef is making his list, the young SS soldier is gathering his list. He reaches the field and runs over to the senior guard patrolling the field, who points out both Mosha and Irena, working near to each other.

The guard, a little out of breath, runs up to them. He thrusts the paper under Mosha's face. She looks up but doesn't say anything.

'Write.'

She just looks at him.

'The choir. I need a list of the choir.'

Mosha looks around at the patrol at the other end of the field.

She just asks one word: 'Why?'

The soldier looks uncomfortable but tells her, 'Commandant Hanke requested it.'

'Do you know why?'

'No, he just told me to get it.'

Mosha looks over at Irena, 'Psssst.' Irena looks up. She waves the sheet of blank paper at her. Irena inches closer until they can talk, although they both keep an eye on the patrol.

'He wants a list of who's in the choir.'

Irena instantly knows who she means. 'Why?' Irena looks at both Mosha and the guard, who shrug in unison.

Mosha asks, 'Do you think it's a good thing or a bad thing?' The women both look at the guard and walk away from him. The young, inexperienced soldier doesn't know whether to follow or not. Luckily for them, he chooses to stay put.

Irena asks her, 'What are you thinking?'

'Do we put more women's names down if it means something good, or if we add more are we condemning more women to death?'

'That's some scary dice to roll.'

'I know – obviously he has no idea who's in the choir, otherwise why would I have to write this list? But if we add more women from the barrack, what will I be doing?'

'But it could mean more food, extra blankets, maybe even different jobs.'

'I have a bad feeling about this.' Mosha makes a snap decision. 'I'm just going to write down who really is in the choir. If it's extra food or blankets for us, we can always share. After everything that's happened, I don't want to be responsible for anything that happens to anyone else.'

'I understand.'

Mosha scribbles down the names of thirty women. She passes the paper over to Irena, who scans it quickly.

'Is that everyone?'

Irena nods, then calls over to the soldier, 'Hey, we're done.' He grabs the paper from her and takes off down the field.

Irena quips, 'He's in a rush.'

'Maybe he needs it urgently as the chef's cooking us up a five-course meal and they need to know how many places to set!' Mosha retorts drily.

Meanwhile, on the other side of the camp, the young soldier makes it back to Josef's house. He knocks on the door and waits for his superior to yell, 'Enter!'

Inside already are Elsa, who stands in front of Josef, and next to her is the main *SS-Oberführer* (Colonel), the next highest ranking officer after the Commandant, and the beast who oversees all the male prisoners.

Josef is on the phone. 'Yes, sir. November 3. I understand.'

He puts down the phone, looks from Elsa to the colonel as the young soldier hands over the list, which Josef puts to one side.

The guard slips out as Josef says, 'It's confirmed. *Aktion Erntefest* is scheduled for November 3. We don't have much time to play with. But Colonel, I need you to get the men to dig some pits as close to the crematorium as possible. We have 18,000 prisoners to execute, and *Führer* Helldorf wants it all done in one day.'

'One day?' Elsa can't contain her surprise.

Josef replies very matter-of-factly, 'Yes, one day. So, most of the prisoners will be shot – it's the quickest and easiest way. The first round will be shot and taken into the crematorium immediately, while the second round will be lined up. It will take longer to burn the bodies than it will to shoot everyone, so we need the pits to keep the bodies in while they are waiting to be burned. Colonel, I'll leave it up to you to decide how many pits you need or how big they will be.

Here is your list of who will be executed. Every single Jew and a few thousand more prisoners who are getting too sick to work efficiently.'

He hands several pages over to the colonel and then looks over at Elsa. 'All of the women will be executed except the women who are members of the choir and a handful of others.'

He pauses to see if Elsa will say anything, but she wisely keeps quiet. He continues: 'The men will be first, starting with the ones from Field V – so we can then take the prisoners to those blocks when they are empty and have them all undress there, as those blocks are closest to the pits. Field V first, then IV, then III, and so forth. The women will go last. But I want everyone out at roll call as usual.'

He hands a list over to Elsa as the colonel asks, 'When on the 3rd are we doing this?'

Josef replies, 'Schedule roll call early for 5 a.m. It will probably take all day to carry this out, so I want to get an early start.'

Elsa and the colonel both reply, 'Yes, sir.'

'Dismissed.'

30

November 1, 1943
It's bitterly cold as the first snow of winter falls heavily across Lublin. The wind whips through the barracks, with some of the huts freezing as they still don't have windowpanes or anything to keep out the cold.

The women huddle up together, trying to stay warm. They all wear every item of clothing and their blankets, but they are still cold. Even sharing body warmth doesn't stop their extremities from going numb or their teeth from chattering.

The two heaters – one placed at either end of the barrack – are no use in these sub-zero temperatures and provide no comfort at all.

The siren blares but most of the women are already awake. In fact, most of them haven't been able to sleep at all. They rise from their beds, shivering. They try jumping up and down, stomping their feet – anything to try and get the feeling back in their fingers and toes.

Irena calls out, 'Can someone look out the window and see if the snow has settled?'

A woman calls back, 'Yes, it's all white outside.'

Irena instructs the women, 'Get your bowls ready.' Several women look baffled but do as they're told.

Irena nods up to Danuta, who calls out, 'Hello! Hello! This is Radio Majdanek. Good morning, ladies. And, yes, it is a good morning! Despite the freezing temperatures and snow outside, this is a wonderful time of year!

'Grab any bowls you may have hidden away and get out outside and fill them with snow. Yes, at last we have clean, fresh water for drinking and cleaning.

'So scoop up as much as you can. Rub that snow on your face and feel refreshed. Eat as much of it as you can. We all know we need to keep hydrated, right?

'However, it's best to stay away from the latrine end of the field. No one wants to eat yellow snow! Am I right, ladies?'

The women rush out of the door and into the snow before the radio broadcast has even finished. They scrabble around, scooping up handfuls of the ice and shovelling it into their mouths, trying to quench their constant thirst.

Some of the younger women lie down in the snow and laugh as they make snow angels. This is the most carefree they have been since they arrived in this godforsaken place. Mosha grabs a handful of snow and puts it on her tongue, letting it melt into liquid before swallowing. She looks around at the women all doing the same and marvels at how something so simple as snow could bring so much joy.

She lets herself smile as she spies Lotte making up a snowball and then launching it at Irena, who is momentarily stunned by the young girl's cheekiness before she gathers up her own snowball and returns fire. Soon there are snowballs flying in all directions, until the sound of gunfire stops them all in their tracks.

They turn and look as several SS guards stand a few yards away. One has his arm raised in the air. He fires his pistol one more time, even though he already has everyone's attention. A female Block Elder steps forward. 'What are you doing?'

Irena speaks for everyone: 'Collecting snow to wash and clean with.'

There are a few sniggers behind her but Irena keeps her eyes locked on the Block Elder and the guns.

The Block Elder can't really say anything as the women are once again collecting the snow, and by now all of the women are out of the barracks doing the same. It's simply not feasible to beat every single one of them, so she simply tells them, 'Enough. Roll call in five minutes.'

'Thank you.'

As the Block Elder turns to go, Irena boldly asks, 'Could we please get a bucket for the snow?'

'A bucket?'

'Yes, buckets for each barrack, so we can put the snow in there to melt. Then we have water, so we can wash ourselves and our clothes in the barrack. It would save us – and you – going to the bathhouse or laundry in this weather.'

The Block Elder briefly considers it. 'I'll see what I can do.'

'Thank you.'

'Now get everyone ready for roll call.'

Irena nods and heads back into the barrack. The minute she steps inside, she's pelted with a dozen snowballs as the women all collapse into laughter. Irena smiles as she shakes the snow from her hair and face.

'Quickly, put your bowls under the bunks out of the way so they won't be kicked over. And quickly grab some breakfast. Roll call is in five minutes.'

A handful of bowls filled with snow are pushed under the bunks out of the way and the women rush out and across the field to grab their fake coffee. They are left pleasantly surprised when this morning it's slightly warmer than usual. Still not piping hot but it's enough to warm their bellies on this cold day.

Word quickly spreads through the women's blocks that *Oberaufseherin* Klein is already in the field. Women gulp down their drinks and dash outside, trying not to bump into each other as they form their orderly lines.

Elsa is wrapped up very warmly with nice leather boots and gloves, a thicker-than-normal black wool uniform, and her hat. She waits until all the women are in line to tell them, 'Today you will be issued with a coat. You may wear this coat while you work in the fields or walk to and from the factory. Once the cold weather is over, you will give this coat back.'

As Elsa speaks, several guards carrying armfuls of coats walk up and down the lines. As one soldier carries the coats, another grabs one off the top of the pile and literally throws it at the prisoner.

None of the coats are really thick or particularly warm but the women are just grateful for an extra layer of clothing. They quickly shrug on whatever they are given, and despite already wearing several layers, most of the outer garments are way too large. Still, they wrap up as best they can and steel themselves to spend a long time at roll call this morning. It's unspoken, but when there's a miscount for the third time and they're still standing in the yard at 9 a.m., they all know it's punishment for this morning's fun snowball fight.

Finally, Elsa is satisfied with the count and lets them head off to begin their workday. It's now almost 10 a.m. but the day is so dismal and depressing, the dawn gaiety has long worn off and the women by this time are wet and cold, their feet soaked through. They might now have a coat but they are all still wearing the basic shoes they were issued when they arrived at the camp.

Those out in the field are in for a miserable day, and by the time they traipse back into camp, their feet are numb, and many also have scrapes on their knees where they've fallen down on the walk back.

As soon as she reaches the barrack, Mosha hobbles inside and over to her bunk. She pulls off her shoes and then her soaking wet stockings. She desperately wants to wring them out but doesn't want to get water all over the floor. But she looks down and realises the melted snow has already overflowed from their bowls and there's water everywhere. It's so cold inside the hut, the water has frozen and turned the floor into an ice rink. Mosha confirms this as she puts her bare feet onto the floor and the freezing ice almost burns her. She whips her feet back up onto the bunk and tucks them inside her coat in a feeble attempt to get warm.

She looks around the barrack. It's complete chaos as the women try to strip off their wet clothes and change into their dry clothes. The problem is they have nowhere to now put the dripping wet clothes and stockings.

Irena stands in the corner talking to Matylda and Danuta. They are furiously nodding and pointing at bunks, women, the door. Danuta jumps up onto her bunk and begins her broadcast:

'Hello, hello, ladies! This is Radio Majdanek. Well, haven't we had a fun day out in the winter wonderland! But now we're back, with cold bellies and wet feet. Be quick and change out of those sexy uniforms and into the dry beige winter fashion.

'As a special treat this evening, we've launched the Camp Majdanek drying station. The two sets of bunks closest to the heater at the far end are available to hang those clothes on and those stockings across. The mattresses will be removed and some lucky ladies are going to get extra padding tonight and an extra body in their bunk! But just think of all that nice additional body heat! Good night, ladies. Tomorrow will be a better – and warmer – day.'

Working as a team, the women move the mattresses and begin laying out the damp clothes on the bunks' wooden slats. They pile up the shoes in front of the heater, hoping they might dry out a little before morning.

It's still a few hours yet before lights out, but it's already pitch black outside and the women need warmth. Without speaking, as one they all turn in for the night, wrap themselves up as best they can and hug each other, not just for warmth but also comfort.

Tonight, Mosha snuggles up to Maria. There's no practising of the piano scales like she usually does. Even if she could feel her fingers, her mind is as numb as her body. She practically has to will herself to sleep. As she drifts off, Mosha has no idea that in just forty-eight hours, she and just a few of the women will have all the blankets they need to keep warm.

31

November 3, 1943

It's early morning a few days later. The women have been on edge since Mosha returned from Josef's hut, but nothing else has happened since. Yesterday was the same as the day before, and the day before that. A little food, just a mouthful or two each, and a harsh workday.

But today something feels different. Music is already playing through the speakers as the women line up for roll call. Usually the music is switched on as they begin their march through the gates to work, but this morning it's filling the 5 a.m. air. It's Tchaikovsky's 'Dance of the Sugar Plum Fairy', the third movement from *The Nutcracker*.

While the women are still getting in lines, Irena cracks, 'Do they want us to dance to work?'

Giggles break out near her, prompting several guards to step forward with guns raised. One of them yells, '*Sei Ruhig*,' and the women quickly quieten down.

Mosha looks around and realises there are more women in the field than usual. As well as the prisoners from all the barracks, all the female political prisoners have been rounded up too, who usually have their own roll call in the SS sector before heading out to the factories.

Elsa strides through the gate with a bullhorn and ascends the platform in front of all the women. She surveys them all, standing in line after line after line, like dominoes ready to fall.

Elsa switches on the bullhorn. 'From today, full rations will be reinstated. And there will be extra rations – for some of you.'

An excited murmur sweeps the crowd. The women look over at Mosha but she refuses to look at any of them; she keeps staring straight ahead at Elsa. She knows there will be a price to pay for this.

Elsa shouts into the bullhorn, 'Quiet!' She waits for the silence. 'If you're tapped on the shoulder, step out of line, follow the Kapos. If you are not tapped on the shoulder, you will wait in line.'

At least a dozen Kapos walk among the women, tapping every two out of four women on the shoulder. These women smile, thinking they have been specially chosen for extra rations. As the women step out, Elsa adds, 'Follow the Kapos. Keep moving. Follow in your lines.'

The women follow them through the gates and they turn left on the path that leads past Fields II, III, IV and their old Field V. The only things beyond those fields are the execution pits and the new crematorium.

As they walk past the men's barracks, the women at the front can see ahead of them and notice that the men's fields are completely empty. There should be thousands of men standing at roll call. But like their own field, there are just a few men here and there, looking dazed. All of a sudden, gunshots fill the air. Not just one or two but a constant barrage of noise. They suddenly realise the old rumours are true, and they know where they are headed – to their deaths.

A few make a run for it but are shot in the back as they flee. The Kapos continue to march the women towards the pits. Many of them are crying. They know they are going to die. They have but one choice: be shot for running away like a coward or be shot while staring down the barrel of a rifle. Some take the first option and step out of line on purpose. They would rather be shot in the back, facing away from the enemy.

But first, they are directed into several blocks in Field V. These buildings are already empty – the men having already taken their death march across the field to their waiting graves.

Once inside the building, the women are ordered to strip naked. Confused, they look around, unsure why they need to do this. Realisation dawns on many of them that the Nazis don't want to waste the clothes they are wearing. They want – no, need – them naked so the next batch of prisoners who arrive will have clothing.

After they have shed their clothes, they stand shivering, huddled together for warmth, but are quickly forced, in groups, out of the blocks, across the frozen field and directed towards a gap that has already been cut in the barbed-wire fence.

The women desperately try not to let their naked flesh touch the fence, but many are left scratched as the SS soldiers herd them through the gap.

Soon the women are standing in front of freshly dug pits, where they are instructed to line up opposite their executors.

These women are face to face with the firing squad. Dozens of SS soldiers, most of them no more than twenty years old. But they all look at the sobbing women with glee. The head SS guard waits until they all have their guns pointed and then yells, 'FIRE!'

Bodies fall, riddled with bullets. The gunshots ring out across the camp, shocking the women waiting in Field I. The women still standing in line look ahead, trying not to react. But as they realise what is happening, many are openly crying while rooted to the spot. They dare not move, not even to wipe away their tears.

The guards walk through the lines again and begin tapping more women on the shoulder. If they weren't sobbing before, they are now.

Elsa tells them, 'Follow the Kapos.' The second batch of women file out of the field.

Just a quarter of the women remain as the others are herded out of the field and towards the pits.

Another round of screams and crying fills the air. The few women left cover their ears, trying to block out the horror.

Elsa raises her bullhorn. 'Unblock your ears. You will listen.' The women reluctantly put their hands down at their sides but keep staring ahead. The gunfire ends, for now. But another batch of women are led out of the field.

Mosha, Celina, Irena, Lotte and the few remaining women wait in line, too shocked to move. Finally, this horrific episode is over. Until Elsa addresses the women once more: 'Your work today is collecting the clothing from Field V and taking it to the warehouse. Now get to work.'

Elsa smiles to herself as she steps off the platform and walks away from the audible sobbing. The women just stand there, too traumatised to move – until the guards point their Gewehr rifles right in their faces.

They turn as one and trudge through the gate towards Field V and the pile of clothes waiting for them inside the blocks.

The women huddle as a group outside the doors, unwilling to be the first to venture inside. One of the guards fires his gun in the air. They all jump at the noise but are still reluctant to face the horror that awaits them. Mosha steps forward, pulls on the door handle, braces herself, but as she flings open the door, it's the smell that overpowers her – a smell of death, urine and human waste.

Many of the clothes are soiled and the smell makes her gag. She tries to pull her shirt up over her mouth as she enters the building. Her eyes begin to water from the stench but she ploughs on. She pulls open the first door; she can't avoid the sight of the clothes her friends were wearing just hours before.

Mosha takes an involuntary step backwards, collides with Celina, who peers over her shoulder. '*Shalom*,' escapes from Celina's lips as she closes her eyes briefly before squeezing Mosha's shoulder. 'Let's do this.'

The sisters enter the room, holding their breaths. They gently approach the clothes, pick them up as though they were made of rare silk. The remaining women follow their lead and enter the barrack, before leaving with armfuls of urine-soaked blouses and skirts.

Several hours later, the women arrive back in the camp after work, line up for roll call. Completely exhausted, the women can barely stand. But it's not just physical exhaustion; they are mentally scarred too as they look around at the few lines of women left.

It all still seems unreal, and after the day's horror, they are all too numb to feel, let alone speak. An eerie silence washes over the compound before music blares out over the loudspeakers.

As the roll call ends, there's a commotion at the end of the camp as several trucks of new inmates arrive, who are herded towards the huts.

As the women watch the new arrivals, Lotte is hard at work in the kitchen preparing a watery broth for dinner. She was pulled out of line earlier to prepare the first food that's not stale bread that the women have had in days.

She hums to herself. Her humming gets louder. Without realising she begins to sing:

Barbed wire, loaded with death
Is drawn around our world.
Above a sky without mercy
Sends frost and sunburn.
Far from us are all joys.

Lotte is so engrossed in the song and work, she doesn't hear Elsa walk up behind her. Elsa quietly stands, listens for a few seconds before she asks, 'What are you singing?'

Lotte jumps, knocks the pot, at least half of the broth spills onto the floor. Lotte stutters, 'N-n-nothing,' as she bends down to clean up the mess.

Elsa holds her arm out. 'Leave it.' As Lotte stands up, Elsa demands to know, 'What was that song?'

Eyes downcast, Lotte replies, 'It was nothing.'

Elsa gives a snort of laughter. 'You're a terrible liar. Who taught you that song?'

Lotte is quiet but defiant. 'No one. I just heard it.'

Elsa doesn't believe her for a second. 'It was Mosha Gebert, wasn't it?'

'No!' insists Lotte.

'You two are always together. You follow her around like a little lost puppy.'

Lotte continues to deny it. 'It wasn't her.'

Elsa tells her, 'We'll see. And don't make any more broth. Just serve what's left in the pan.'

But as Elsa leaves, Lotte gets down on her knees, tries to scoop up the broth from the floor to put it back in the pot.

32

Several days pass. The women keep their heads down. The shock still hasn't worn off. They haven't spoken about it; no one wants to bring it up or talk about what happened.

So they work in silence, and in the evenings they just lie on their bunks. There's been no singing or choir practice. No one feels like singing anymore. The new prisoners that have arrived keep to themselves; no one is in the mood to make friends.

The women wearily return to camp as dusk falls. Mosha trudges along with the rest of the exhausted prisoners. She's only a few feet inside the gates when an SS soldier calls to her, 'You. Come here.'

Mosha doesn't hear him – she's still having trouble hearing anything out of her right ear – so she keeps walking. The soldier screams, '5391.'

Still she doesn't hear. The soldier pushes through the women, grabs Mosha, pulls her out of the line and to one side. Mosha looks surprised but doesn't resist. None of the other women react; they know by now to just keep walking.

Mosha is marched across the yard to the Block, AKA the Grand Piano. The soldier stops her next to it. 'Stand there.' Mosha does as she's told. She shivers as the late November evening turns colder.

The loudspeaker blares, 'ROLL CALL.' The women line up so they face Mosha. Some strain to see, especially the new prisoners; others look at the ground. Most know what's to come – and it isn't good.

Elsa strides across the camp. She stands next to Mosha, a smile on her face. One of the SS soldiers hands her a bullhorn. Elsa clears her throat, takes her time before she announces, 'I know this woman has been teaching you to sing.' Elsa pauses for effect but none of the women react.

She continues: 'She has been teaching banned songs. You will all witness this punishment because you have all taken part in the crime. But this Jew is the one being punished because she is the teacher.'

Elsa casts her eyes across the lines. No one will meet her stare. Elsa nods with satisfaction and signals the Kapos. Two of them step forward. They each take one of Mosha's arms, lead her to the Block. They push her down onto the semi-circular board.

Mosha doesn't struggle. She's resigned to her fate. She knows if she struggles, the punishment will not only be bad for her but worse for the others. So, she puts her feet behind a special board at the rear of the table, then lays down on her stomach.

The two Kapos hold her arms, twisted back between her shoulder blades. Elsa steps up to the Block. Another Kapo hands her a large truncheon-like stick. She leans in close so only Mosha can hear her. 'See, you do get to play your stupid grand piano. But you play it my way.'

Elsa steps back. Raises her arm up high. Brings down the stick across Mosha's back. Mosha can't help but cry out, 'Arrgghhhhhh.' The stick comes down again, again. By the fifth time, Mosha's cries get louder. As the seventh blow rains down, a sweet melodical voice rises from the crowd:

Standing firm in a great and difficult time
Is a people dedicated to the struggle for their King.

More voices begin to join in to sing 'Fest Steht' (Stand Fast). Soon all the female prisoners' voices ring out as one:

He teaches us to fight and win,
Bright is the eye and calm the blood;
Their sword is the truth; they wield it well:
What serves the enemy all its lies?

Mosha's cries turn to laughter as Elsa strikes her for the tenth time. Elsa is beyond furious. She blindly brings the baton down with such force it breaks.

Suddenly a male voice explodes: 'What the hell is going on here?'

Elsa whips around to see Josef standing just three feet away. She immediately drops the broken stick. At the same time, the singing stops.

Elsa tells him, 'Punishment.'

Josef raises an eyebrow, 'For what?'

'Singing.'

Josef looks at Mosha, who is now slumped over the Block. 'Singing? But the prisoners are encouraged to sing while they work. You know the prohibition of music in all camps has been lifted by the *Führer*.'

Elsa presses home her point: 'Yes, sir. But she was teaching them banned songs.'

'You heard her?'

Elsa has to admit, 'No, but…'

Josef looks at her with contempt. 'Then how do you know it was her?'

'I know it was.'

Josef turns to Mosha; it takes every ounce of his willpower not to reach out and touch her. His hands ball into fists as he snaps, 'Untie her. Now.'

From the tone in his voice, Elsa knows not to challenge him. 'Yes, sir.' She nods to the Kapos, who step forward and untie Mosha as Josef takes a few steps back out of the way.

Mosha slumps to the ground. She can barely move, her back is on fire, but no one dares move to help. Josef finally moves over to her. He bends down and checks she's still breathing. As his hand touches her wrist to check for a pulse, Mosha whimpers slightly. His hand reaches out to caress her cheek but he remembers where he is, checks himself.

Josef stands up and walks back over to Elsa. He stands close so no one else can hear as he leans in to her. 'Have her taken to the infirmary. Then I want to see you in my hut.'

Elsa nods. 'Yes, sir.' As Josef walks away, Elsa realises everyone is now watching. Eyes that were previously cast to the floor watch eagerly to see how Elsa will react.

'Get her out of here.'

As two Kapos pick Mosha up, the singing starts again, defiant, in harmony. Elsa snaps her head around but this time no one stops.

Innocent in their cells, robbed of their freedom!
Scornfully the enemies raise up their heads:
They would like to rule over us.

Elsa takes two steps forward. Her hand goes to her belt before she realises her broken baton lies on the floor several feet away.

She stares down the women for several seconds, then storms off in the direction of Josef's house.

33

Moments later, Josef stands over Elsa, who sits nervously in a chair inside his hut. He explodes, 'What the hell were you thinking?'

While his anger worries her, Elsa believes she was doing the right thing. 'She needed to be punished.'

But Josef is furious that she completely ignored his instructions. 'I told you she wasn't to be harmed.'

Elsa thinks she can make him see reason, see that she was right. 'I needed to make an example of her. The other women look up to her. They need to know she's not untouchable.'

Josef takes a deep breath, reigns in his anger. 'She's not. But there are other ways to punish her. Ways that won't harm her physically.'

A defiant Elsa tells him, 'Everything you have done so far has not worked.'

Josef snarls, 'How dare you question me?'

He crosses to the other side of the room, away from Elsa. He clenches, then unclenches his fists several times. He struggles not to strike something. As much as he wants to lash out, he won't strike Elsa.

He turns to her. 'Celina. Her sister.'

Elsa immediately understands. She nods. 'What do you want me to do?'

'Move her. To the SS quarters. She will service the soldiers.'

Elsa doesn't understand this. 'But she's Jewish! They won't touch her.'

Josef smiles and explains, 'She's not for any of the officers. Send her to the regular soldiers. They won't care.'

Elsa smiles. 'My pleasure.'

She gets up to leave, but as she passes Josef, he grabs her arm. 'I don't forget.'

Elsa searches his eyes. She needs to know what this Jewish *klafte* has that she doesn't.

Josef tells her, 'Don't ever touch her again. You have a problem, you come to me.'

Elsa nods. 'Yes, sir.'

He releases her arm. Elsa rubs at the red marks he's left on her arm as she slips out of the room. Josef goes to the gramophone and puts on a record.

It's Wagner's 'Ride of the Valkyries', the operatic story of the Valkyries, mythic figures in Norse mythology who take half of the warriors slain in battle to Valhalla, a celebratory hall of the afterlife where they will prepare for the final apocalyptic battle, Ragnarok.

Josef sinks down into the chair and begins to pleasure himself. He closes his eyes. Images of Mosha wearing the pink dress float around his head. He pictures her spread across the Block and his need becomes more and more urgent.

He reaches his crescendo at the same time as the music.

34

The infirmary is only marginally cleaner than the rest of the camp. Disease breeds here rather than being stamped out. Anyone who enters the infirmary rarely makes it out alive.

Mosha lies on her stomach on a single dirty bed, a sheet draped over her. Celina sits next to her, holds her hand as she shivers. A male doctor approaches. Without saying anything, he whips off the sheet and pulls Mosha's top upwards to expose her back.

She tries not to scream out from the pain as the top at first sticks to the large red bloody welts across her back, then as the doctor pulls harder, rips off some of her skin. She grips Celina's hand.

The doctor peers down at Mosha's mangled and bruised back. He doesn't touch it or ask her any questions. Instead, he simply declares, 'All she needs is rest.'

An outraged Celina almost yells from frustration, 'That's it?' As the doctor shrugs she adds, 'Is there nothing you can give her for the pain?'

The doctor sighs, 'It's just a bruise. She'll be fine in a day or so.'

Celina can hardly believe what she's hearing. 'Just a bruise? Look at the blood. There are welts on her back from the whipping. She can hardly move!'

The doctor looks at Mosha dispassionately. 'I've seen worse.' That's not a lie. There has been much worse in the camp, but that doesn't quell Celina.

'There must be something you can do.'

Again, the doctor just shrugs. 'I have nothing. Take her back.'

But Celina is determined to get some kind of treatment for her sister. 'There's no way she can walk. She's got to stay here.'

The doctor takes his hand, presses down hard on Mosha's back. She screams. 'See? She can feel me touching her. That means it's just a bruise.'

Completely livid, Celina stands, squares up to the doctor, but before she can say or do anything, a hand clamps down

157

on her shoulder. She spins around and comes face to face with Elsa.

Behind Elsa are two SS soldiers. Elsa nods to them. 'Take her away.'

Celina struggles to get free as she resists. 'No! No!' But the soldiers grab Celina and try to pull her towards the door. She grabs at Mosha's hand and holds on, but when Mosha cries out in pain, Celina drops her hand.

She fights with everything she has as the soldiers drag her out of the building. She's screaming and yelling. She's past caring what happens to herself; she's being combative for Mosha. But it doesn't do either of them any good.

One of the soldiers hits Celina in the back of the head with his rifle butt. Knocked out, she drops to the floor. The soldiers don't bother to pick her up; instead, they just drag her through the mud to the SS quarters.

Meanwhile, with a wave of her hand, Elsa dismisses the doctor, who is more than happy to retreat to his office at the end of the infirmary.

Now alone with her nemesis, Elsa moves closer to the bed and looks down at Mosha, her body a broken mess. Elsa looks around to make sure the infirmary is completely deserted. Her hand reaches out and she quickly pokes Mosha's back with her finger. It isn't hard, and Mosha tries not to cry out, but the pain is too much.

Elsa pokes her again and again. 'You think he saved you. But you've only made it worse. Nothing can save you now.'

Mosha turns her head and looks Elsa directly in the eye. Elsa's lips are moving but Mosha doesn't hear her. She closes her eyes, shuts Elsa out. Despite several more pokes, each one harder than the last, Mosha keeps her eyes shut tight.

Elsa finally gets bored after getting no reaction. She wipes her bloody finger on the sheet, then turns on her heel, strides out of the infirmary.

35

Inside the SS quarters, a half-hearted attempt has been made to turn one room at the end of the hall into a place of comfort – and pleasure. But the cheap, garish blankets just add to the depression that hangs over the room like an oppressive shroud.

Celina sits scrunched up on the floor in the corner, her arms pulling her knees tight into her chest. A young SS soldier opens the door, walks in while unbuttoning his jacket. He grins at Celina while pointing to the bed.

Tears slip down her cheeks as she stands, drops her skirt to the floor.

As Celina silently weeps into the darkness, Mosha lies in her own kind of darkness as she drifts in and out of consciousness. She lies face down on the bed, still unable to bear anything touching her back.

She has no idea when Josef enters the room and crosses over to the bed. He leans in close, hovers over her, careful not to touch her.

But the medals on his jacket accidentally brush across Mosha's shoulder blade. She involuntarily flinches and moans. Josef leans in closer and whispers in her ear, '*Mutter.*'

Then he picks up her hand, caresses her fingers. She stirs again but doesn't wake as he places her hand back on the bed.

Josef sits in a chair in the corner, just watches her sleep.

36

Several days later, Mosha enters the barrack flanked by two Kapos. She's stiff as a board, moves at a snail's pace and winces with every step. She's determined to walk on her own, but every few yards, one of the Kapos pushes her ahead.

Mosha tries not to stumble and makes her way to her bunk. As she reaches it, the Kapos stand and wait as she eases herself down onto it. One Kapo speaks loud enough for everyone to hear: 'You've got off easy lately. But tomorrow you'll be back in the field.'

Mosha just looks at her, shrugs and then points to her ear. This time the Kapo shouts at her, 'Tomorrow. Fields!'

All the other women pretend to be doing something else, anything else. Except Irena, who pushes past the Kapos to stand next to Mosha's bunk. Irena says, 'She can't work in that condition.'

The Kapo grins, 'Orders from the Commandant himself. She either plays for him or works in the field. She picked the field herself.'

Irena shakes her head at Mosha. She will never understand this crazy, stubborn woman. As Irena walks away, the Kapo look down at Mosha, whose face is now slick with sweat.

The Kapo shouts again, 'Make sure you're at roll call!' Both Kapos turn in unison and march out of the barracks. Irena returns to the bunk with food and a sheet. She places the meagre piece of bread on Mosha's bunk. Mosha pushes it away but Irena gestures for her to eat.

Mosha smiles up at her and admits, 'I can hear perfectly well in my left ear and now a little in the right one too. I pretend I can't hear at all just to mess with them. But if you speak on my left side, I can hear you just fine.'

Irena moves to Mosha's left side, unsure how to tell her. Mosha looks around, suddenly realising there is someone missing. 'Where's Celina?'

'I'm so sorry.'

Mosha chokes back tears. 'She's not—'

Irena stops her. 'No, as far as we know, she's alive.'

'Where is she?' Irena shifts uncomfortably as Mosha asks more forcefully, 'Where is she?'

Irena takes a breath. 'We heard she'd been taken to the SS quarters.'

A furious Mosha replies, 'That bastard. I'll kill him.'

Irena places her hand gently on Mosha's arm. 'You can barely move but you're going to kill him?'

Mosha looks at her and they both start to laugh. 'You know what I mean.'

Irena tells her, 'I do, but you can't think about it right now. You need to eat, get your strength back. Then we decide what to do.'

Mosha nods, blinks away the tears. She takes a small bite of bread and tries to chew, before admitting, 'It even hurts to eat.'

Irena adds, 'I know, but it will hurt even more tomorrow when you're out in the field.'

Mosha can't swallow the bread, it's stuck in her throat and she starts to cough. Irena yells out, 'Water!' and a bowl of melted snow is passed over to the bunk. Mosha sips on it, finally manages to get the bread down.

'I can't eat any more. It's too painful.'

Irena breaks off a piece of bread from the middle, the softest part, and puts it in Mosha's mouth as she coaxes, 'Just try a little bit more.' Mosha slowly chews and chews and chews, trying not to show the pain on her face, but with every breath, she's in agony. Irena waits until she finally swallows again before she adds, 'Take your shirt off.' Mosha just looks at her, bewildered.

Irena tells her, 'Take it off. I need to look at you. You've had no proper treatment while you were in the infirmary. Maybe I can do something to help.'

Irena carefully helps Mosha out of her shirt. Underneath is a threadbare vest. Irena gently lifts it and gasps at the swirl of blue and purple bruises that cover Mosha's back and sides. Thankfully, the welts have started to heal over, but her back still looks a mess. 'This is going to hurt but I need to see how many ribs are broken.'

Mosha takes a deep breath as Irena's fingers probe her bruised back and sides. Irena tells her, 'I can feel at least three broken ribs. You're lucky they haven't punctured a lung.'

Mosha retorts, 'Lucky?' She winces as Irena's fingers probe a little deeper. Mosha grabs her hand, stops her. 'How do you know about this?'

Irena sighs. 'I trained as a doctor.'

Mosha looks at her incredulously. 'You were a doctor?'

'No. I trained as one. But I was a woman, so I became a nurse. My husband was the doctor.'

There's still a slight resentment in her voice. Mosha picks up on it. 'I'm so sorry.'

Irena brushes aside her. 'Don't be. I learned all I needed to know. I helped run the practice with my husband. We had a good life.'

Mosha hesitates, then asks, 'Where is he now?'

Almost matter-of-factly, Irena replies, 'Dead.'

Mosha looks at Irena's face. There's no emotion; she's intent on fixing Mosha's ribs. She picks up the sheet, tears it into long strips. Irena holds up one of the strips. 'I need to bind your ribs. It will help them heal faster. But I'm going to need you to raise your arms up.'

Mosha slowly raises her arms above her head as Irena wraps the strips of sheets around Mosha's body. She pulls them tight. Mosha tries not to cry out.

Irena puts Mosha's arms back down to her sides. 'We'll have to wrap them every morning and night. But it will help.'

Mosha nods but the tears well up. Irena asks, 'Are the strips too tight?'

Mosha shakes her head, takes one of the leftover strips from the bed, dabs at her eyes. 'Celina.'

Irena leans in close, gives her a gentle hug, careful not to squeeze too tight. 'You're here, she's there. But she's alive. If he kills Celina, he's got no leverage over you. Just keep that thought.'

Irena lets her go, looks at the makeshift bandages and smiles. 'Not too bad for a nurse!'

Mosha manages a weak smile. 'Thank you.'

The next day, Mosha's in line for roll call as ordered. She slowly walks out with the rest of her campmates but she's struggling. She manages the mile walk out to the field. With every breath it's like a knife stabbing her in the side, but she refuses to show the pain. She won't give the soldiers the satisfaction of showing weakness.

But they can see it as Mosha struggles to pick up the rocks. The determination on her face is mingled with sweat as she grabs a rock but fails to lift it. She quickly moves on to a smaller one and manages to move it into her basket.

A guard strolls past and openly laughs at her. Mosha pretends she hasn't heard him and carries on picking up the tiniest of rocks.

Once he's passed, Mosha dares to take a break. As she stands upright, a man, Otto Schepps, tentatively approaches her. He's so skinny he weighs no more than Mosha, but he picks up rocks she can't and puts them in her basket.

Mosha reaches out to stop him, winces from the pain. 'Please stop.'

Otto ignores her pleas, carries on filling up her basket. He tells her, 'As long as they get their quota they won't care.'

Otto moves closer to Mosha, bends down to pick up a rock. Mosha also bends down, so her left ear is close to Otto. 'I have a message for you. From Celina.'

Mosha tries not to show her surprise. 'How?'

Otto tells her, 'My sister cleans the SS quarters.' He looks around to make sure the guard is still out of earshot. 'Celina says not to think about her.'

Mosha chokes back tears. 'Does she…' She can't get the words out. 'Does she have to…'

Otto lays his hand on her arm in comfort. 'We all know what happens there. I'm sorry. But my sister said she sings. A lot. She's been teaching the other women there songs too.'

Mosha looks worried. 'She shouldn't do that. It will get her into even more trouble.'

Otto laughs. 'Do you think Celina would listen to anyone if they told her to stop?'

Mosha smiles and admits, 'No.'

Otto continues, 'Besides, the soldiers have heard her sing and ask her to as well. She won't get into trouble while she's singing for them too.'

Mosha says, 'I hope so, as trouble seems to follow her around!'

Otto adds, 'Her message was, "Tell Mosha I sing the songs Mother sang when we were children."'

Now Mosha lays her hand on Otto's arm. 'Thank you. That's a huge comfort to me, knowing music is finally a comfort to her.'

Otto fills Mosha's basket as she begins to hum the lullaby 'Ach Spij Kochanie' (Ah Sleep Baby).

Several hours later, Mosha lays on her bunk, the other women bustling around. Lotte comes over. Mosha nods, sits up slowly. Lotte kneels in front of her, attentive, ready to learn.

'This is a lullaby my mother used to sing to me and Celina when we were young girls.' Lotte smiles, claps her hands like an excited child as Mosha begins to sing:

Ah sleep, baby.
If the star of heaven you want – you will get.

Meanwhile, over in the SS block, Celina is in bed, under the covers. She's naked. A young soldier strips off, gets into bed with her. He rolls on top of her. Celina turns her head so she doesn't have to look at him.

The soldier demands, '*Singen! Singen!*'

As he pumps away, Celina begins to sing the lullaby:

Ah sleep, baby.
If the star of heaven you want – you will get.

The Gebert sisters might be separated by one man's hatred, and a fence, but something deep inside still connects them. As Mosha sings the lullaby to Lotte:

What do you want, let me know.
I can give you everything I can.
So why do not you want to sleep?

Celina also sings the lines:

Ah sleep because that's it.
The moon yawns and it will fall asleep.

Unknowingly, they switch back and forth, reciting the words they would sing together with their mother Eva in another time and another place.

Mosha:

And when morning comes,
The moon will be shameful,
That he fell asleep, not you.

Then Celina:

There were two kittens.
Aaaa, aaaa
Grey-bure, grey-bure both.

Mosha raises her voice as more women join Lotte to learn the song:

Ah sleep, because at night,
When the stars get golden in the sky.

Celina's voice cracks as she closes her eyes to shut out her surroundings:

All children, even bad ones,
They are asleep. And you one, just did not.

Celina finishes the lullaby as the soldier finishes his business. He grunts. Rolls off her. Celina tears up. She angrily wipes them away. Turns over, faces away from the soldier, who gets dressed as she stares blankly at the wall.

Mosha finishes her lullaby and pats Lotte on the shoulder, then shoos her away. She gently lies down on her bunk. In a mirror image of Celina, she turns away from everyone else, faces the wall. Mosha closes her eyes. Pulls her blanket closer. But Celina rolls back over, throws open her blanket. A different soldier climbs into the bed with her.

37

Christmas 1943
The days are getting shorter and colder, but Mosha has healed well. She's back in the fields working in the bitter weather, but being outside clears her mind, and if she's kept busy it gives her less time to think about Celina.

Mosha and Irena stand in the freezing rain as the remaining women exit through the gate. Elsa motions for them to come closer to the platform. They approach her, both wondering what they have done this time.

Elsa informs them, 'Your silly little choir will sing tonight for the Commandant and the SS soldiers. A little concert for Christmas.'

Mosha opens her mouth to protest but is quickly elbowed by Irena, who says, 'Of course. Are there any particular songs the Commandant would like to hear?'

Elsa just waves her hand impatiently. 'Something festive, I don't know.'

'Carols?'

'Anything, as long as you remove any reference to Jesus or Jews.'

Mosha and Irena keep quiet as Elsa thinks for a minute. 'Ahhh yes, you'd better know the official version of "Hohe Nacht der klaren Sterne,"' (Exalted Night of the Clear Stars).

Irena ventures, 'Do we have permission to practise this afternoon while working? I need to make sure the younger girls know the new versions.'

'Yes, yes.'

'And would you like us to wear our regular clothes?'

Elsa looks them up and down, barely disguising the disgust on her face. 'I will have some clothes brought to the barracks from the warehouse later on for you to wear.'

'Thank you.'

'You better make me look good. I told him I heard you practising and that your choir was good – better than the one at Auschwitz.'

Irena smiles. 'Oh, but we are.'

Elsa rolls her eyes and strides out of the gates towards her own hut in the SS sector, out of the rain and into the dry. Mosha and Irena are escorted through the pouring rain to the field. A guard walks behind them but takes no notice as they lean in close to chat, with Mosha furiously asking, 'Why did you ask about what to sing?'

'Look, we're going to have to sing no matter what, so we might as well get it right. The women deserve a little reward at Christmas, and if we do a good job and he's pleased, we might get a decent meal out of it. Do you know the Hitler version of "Silent Night"?'

'No. There's a new version?'

'A special Nazi version. We heard about it last Christmas. They changed a lot of carols. Orders came down from the top that there had to be no reference to God, Christ or religion at all.'

'What?'

'Oh, and that's not all. Their favourite carol she just mentioned? They even changed that and replaced all the traditional Christian themes with their crazy Nazi racial ideologies. You know he's going to want to hear that one for sure.'

'I don't want to sing for him. Or any of them. They won't appreciate it. And besides, I hate stupid Christmas carols!'

'You've got worse things to worry about than singing carols. What if he demands you play? In front of everyone?'

'He won't.'

'How can you be so sure?'

'His perverse view is that I belong to him and no one else. He won't want anyone else to see or hear me playing. He believes that's just a right for him.'

'He's that sick?'

'I told you. He's twisted. He's got this bizarre idea that I'm his and once I play, I'm going to fall in love with him and we're going to live happily ever after with me playing for him every night in his tiny little house.'

'He wants to play happy families with you even though you're Jewish? I thought he was a true believer?'

'Oh, believe me, he is! But in his sick mind, my talent cancels out my Jewishness. He told me that someone who plays like me, has passion like me, is not really Jewish, and can be cleansed, not by death, but by loving him and following his orders.'

Irena pretends to throw up. The two women giggle. Irena adds, 'Let's just hope you're right. The last thing we need is a scene in front of everyone.'

'I know. But there'll be a scene anyway if we don't teach them these new carols.'

With a look of determination on their faces, they approach the unsuspecting choir.

Hours later, the two women and the rest of the choir are standing in the barrack eyeing a pile of clothes. They begin to pick through them, trying to find something that might actually fit them.

Most of the clothes are sparkly, satin or silk gowns, and all are either red or green – very festive.

Mosha quips, 'We're all going to look like Christmas baubles!'

Lotte asks, 'Should we all wear the same colour?'

Mosha shrugs but Irena insists, 'Just find something that fits you if you can. It doesn't matter what colour it is!'

The women dive deeper into the pile, pulling out a variety of dresses. Mosha holds up a particularly revealing red gown with a low-cut neckline and thigh slit. 'Someone was actually arrested wearing this?'

The women laugh as they eventually find some more modest outfits and get changed. They look more like a cabaret act than a choir, but Irena nods her approval. 'They'll love it.'

One of the women pipes up, 'I'm not worried about what we look like. What if we can't remember the words?'

Mosha calms her. 'We've been practising all afternoon. You know this. Just follow my lead.'

Helena replies, 'It's fine for you – it's like you have a photographic memory, you remember everything.'

Mosha laughs. 'That's not a photographic memory, that's years and years of studying, eight hours a day with my mother standing over me with a cane to slap my fingers if I read a piece of music wrong or played the wrong note!'

Irena quips, 'Well, it's the same principle here. Get it wrong, get a beating!' The dark humour sets the women off into peals of laughter before Irena pulls them up. 'Come on, we need to finish getting concert-ready!'

There's also a pile of shoes next to the clothes, mainly high heels. Lotte grabs a pair and squeezes her feet into them and then tries to walk in her first ever pair of stilettos. She totters up and down the aisle between the bunks. She's anything but graceful and looks more like a five-year-old playing dress-up in her mother's shoes. She almost topples over and narrowly misses twisting her ankle.

'How do you wear these?'

'With lots of practice,' Maria informs her.

'Well, I'm sticking to my regular work shoes. There's no way I can walk in these!'

A couple of the older women grab some heels and try them on. One of them does a twirl as she remarks, 'I never thought I'd feel like a woman again.'

They all admire each other and adjust their dresses just as *Oberaufseherin* Klein bangs open the barrack door. She looks them over but doesn't say anything and just gestures for them to head out.

Thankfully, it's only a short walk out of the gates of Field I and onto the paved road to the SS sector. The rain has also stopped and the women feel almost cheerful as they embark on the short journey to their first ever concert.

As they approach the SS sector, Elsa steers them to the largest hut, where there's a loud, rambunctious noise. It definitely sounds like a party. The choir arrives at the door and waits for Elsa to head in first. As the door swings open, they get their first glimpse of what life is like on the other side of the war.

While their hut is barren with just rows and rows of bunks, this hut is drowning in opulence. Even without the Christmas decorations draped around the room, it's clear the SS are living a much more hedonistic lifestyle than their prisoners.

This is the SS 'entertainment' hut, and everything inside is geared towards providing comfort and enjoyment for the soldiers. Sumptuous sofas and armchairs adorn the room. There's a gramophone and a radio on a table against one wall to provide music and news. Another table is filled with more food than all the prisoners get fed in one day. There's German sausage, tins of sardines and herrings, and more bread than Mosha has ever seen in her life.

And bottles of vodka. Lots and lots of bottles of vodka. By the sounds of the shouting and laughter, there's already been a hefty consumption of alcohol. The soldiers are well on their way to being drunk, although some of the younger ones, who barely look out of puberty, are there already.

Some of them are playing cards; others sit around in groups, regaling each other with the best beating they've given a prisoner or, in their eyes, the best punishment they've handed down to some 'deserving stinking Jew'. They try to out-boast each other, all in the name of 'good fun'.

Observing it all from his chair in the far corner is Josef, sipping on a large glass of Göring-Schnapps, also known as Jägermeister. He looks on with drunken pride. These are his men; they are a 'good lot' as far as he is concerned. They do their jobs well, follow his orders, and everything is running well in his camp. They deserve to let off steam, have some entertainment; they've earned it. And so has he. He downs his glass and refills it almost to the top again. A warm glow spreads over him, and he's not sure if it's the alcohol or the fact that Mosha has just entered the room.

Josef has spied the choir as they timidly make their way into the room and stand in a cluster by the door. Elsa scans the room for him but he's already up and out of his seat and heading towards them. He nods his approval and gestures for the women to follow him to the far end of the hut, where a space has been cleared for them.

To get to their performance area, the women have to walk the gauntlet. The soldiers reach out, touch them, grope them, grab at them, but they dare not complain. Wolf whistles fill the air; lewd comments are thrown at them. But there are no reprimands, just good-natured laughter, even from Josef and Elsa.

The women finally make it to their 'stage'. They line up as practised. Mosha can feel Josef's eyes boring into her but she refuses to look at him. She busies herself with making sure the women are ready.

She stands in front of the choir like a conductor, but with her back to Josef. He tries to will her to turn around but she's focused on her girls. She's as proud of them as Josef is of his soldiers.

They begin with Hans Baumann's 'Hohe Nacht der klaren Sterne'. A huge smile spreads over Josef's face as he realises the women are singing the correct lyrics. Soon the soldiers are joining in, drunkenly singing along and almost drowning out the choir.

Mosha tries not to let her annoyance show as the women push on with 'Silent Night' next. To try to calm things down, she instructs the women to sing the hymn 'Unto Us a Time Has Come' – again, with all references to Jesus removed.

This quietens down the soldiers for a couple of verses, but they soon start chanting, 'Carols, carols, carols.' Mosha flicks her eyes over to Elsa, who is standing to the left of the choir. She looks just as annoyed as Mosha does but it's not over the soldiers or the carols. She's watching Josef watch Mosha.

Mosha mouths, 'One more?' to Irena, who nods. Mosha turns, keeping her eyes straight ahead, and announces to the room, 'This one I think you all know: "Jingle Bells".' This one sets the room alight. The soldiers stand and sing along loudly, clinking their glasses together. Mosha briefly closes her eyes. If it wasn't 1943 and she wasn't in Majdanek, she imagines she could be in a bar or café celebrating a happy Christmas with family and friends.

But when she opens her eyes again, reality comes flooding back. She chokes back tears and sees several of the women are also experiencing memories from long ago, memories of happier times with their families.

They finish the song and all give a little bow. The soldiers are yelling and screaming, 'More, more!' Mosha looks to Elsa, who steps forward and tries to calm them down.

'Just one more. It may be Christmas for you, but these Jews still have work to do tomorrow.'

Elsa steps away, this time taking a seat next to Josef. But he ignores her, his face trained on Mosha and the choir. This time, they opt for a more sombre song and begin the refrain of 'Wisst ihr noch, wie es geschehen' (Do You Remember How It Happened). The beautiful melody quietens down the soldiers, who become almost mesmerised as the women sing:

Do you remember how it happened?
We will always tell:
As we once saw the star
In the middle of the dark night,
In the middle of the dark night.

There was silence around the herd.
And suddenly there was a glow

And a singing above the earth,
That the child was born.

There's barely a dry eye in the house as the choir reaches the end of the song. Just moments ago, these raucous soldiers were behaving like they were in a brothel, but now they all sit sombre, reflecting inwards.

Josef stands, gives a barely perceptible bow to Mosha but makes the acknowledgement, 'Thank you.'

The choir are surprised by the thanks, with Irena muttering under her breath, 'Well, I guess it is Christmas.'

Elsa begins to usher them from the stage. They look longingly at the table of food as they pass by. Most of the food will go untouched and most likely be thrown away in the morning. If they're lucky, they might get some of the bread, once it's gone stale, but for tonight they're getting no reward for their concert.

Mosha lets them all go ahead of her and brings up the rear as they file out, but as she passes by Josef, he grips her arm. It's not a death grip but it's enough to stop her. Mosha stands and waits. He leans in and slurs so softly that only she can hear, 'I look forward to a private concert soon.'

She tries not to show her revulsion, but Josef is so drunk he wouldn't notice anyway. He lets her go, watches as she runs to catch up with the others, then pours himself another drink and slumps back into his chair as the soldiers become rowdy once more. Outside the hut, the women walk back to their hut in silence. It's only once inside, when they're alone, do they hug each other in triumph.

They congratulate Mosha and each other and begin chattering away about their performance, the soldiers and even the food. Mosha wanders over to her bunk and sits down. She smiles as the women laugh and recall how one soldier almost ruined 'Silent Night' with his off-key singing.

Irena joins Mosha on her bunk. 'Well, that went better than I expected.'

Mosha agrees. 'We got out of there unscathed!'

'For a minute there I thought the soldiers were going to rush the stage and take over! But the Commandant seemed pleased. What did he say to you?'

'He was too drunk to do anything tonight but he wants a private concert.'

'Of course he does.'

Mosha changes the subject. 'Did you see all the food? I would've happily sung "Hitler is God" just to get a bite of that herring!'

Irena reaches down into the cleavage of her dress and pulls out a sausage. 'It's not a herring but…'

Mosha gasps, 'How on earth did you…'

Irena laughs, 'Klein was marching out the front door, the Commandant was busy whispering sweet nothings in your ear and everyone else was too drunk to care!'

She reaches in and pulls out a second and third sausage. 'I've learned a few things in my time here!'

Mosha flings her arms around Irena. 'You're amazing.'

Irena stands up and waves the sausages in the air. 'Ladies, happy Christmas!'

38

The nights are finally starting to get a little shorter as the spring of 1944 edges closer. Mosha sits on her bunk as the last of the daylight strains through the barrack window. There's still a chill in the air and she grasps a thick blanket around her as she runs scales with Lotte and a few other women.

Leah, a scrawny woman in her thirties, rushes in. 'Mosha? Where's Mosha?'

Mosha waves her arm in the air and calls out, 'Here!'

Leah runs over, pulls a bundle out from underneath her shirt. She puts it in Mosha's hands. 'From your sister.'

Mosha turns the package over and over in her hands. 'How?'

Maria tuts at her, 'You know better than to ask that.'

The women now crowd around; they're more excited than Mosha to find out what's in the package. Deep down, Mosha knows this can only mean one thing: trouble.

But when she opens the bundle, a treasure trove of goodies spills out onto the bunk: bread, cheese, coffee granules.

Mosha scoops everything up and tosses the package onto the table. The other women dive on it excitedly and share it. For a minute, Mosha just sits there. Tears well in her eyes.

One of the women scornfully asks, 'What's wrong with you now? Can't you ever be happy?'

Mosha angrily jumps up, snatches a piece of cheese out of the woman's hand. 'You have no idea what she's had to do for this! And you don't care! All you think about is yourself. You are all so selfish!'

The woman tries to snatch the cheese back but Mosha holds it out of her reach. The woman shoves her. 'Give it to me.'

Mosha shoves her back. 'Never. You don't deserve it. None of you do.'

By now, most of the women have stopped what they are doing and just stare at Mosha and the woman, although one or two discreetly try to shove a piece of bread or cheese into their pockets. With Mosha watching the women watching her, she doesn't see the woman lunge for the cheese and is taken by surprise when the woman wrestles it out of her hand.

Mosha doesn't try to take it back. Instead, she looks around at everyone; most of them are embarrassed and look at the floor or somewhere else, anywhere else, rather than directly at Mosha. One or two have the courage to meet her gaze.

Mosha is furious at their behaviour. 'I am ashamed. Ashamed that Celina is doing awful things in that awful place so that we can eat. You should also be ashamed. What has she had to do for this? How many men for just a piece of bread? Five? Ten? Yet you don't think about that, you just grab the food.'

Some of the women start to look abashed. One or two put pieces of bread back on the table. Irena steps up. 'Mosha, you can't think that way. It will drive you mad.'

Mosha replies, 'Don't you think I'm already mad? Mad at Celina for being in that place. Mad at him. Mad at myself. It's all I can think about.'

'Stop it right now. Celina is alive and is selflessly doing all she can to help us.'

'But I can't stop thinking about her. All those soldiers…'

Irena steps forward, takes Mosha's face in her hands, looks deep into her eyes. 'You have to put it from your mind.'

'How can I? Every time I close my eyes, all I see is Celina being—'

All of a sudden, there's a commotion at the barrack door. Women scatter, shove bread and cheese in their mouths, pockets, anywhere they can, anywhere out of sight. A Kapo appears, approaches Mosha. 'The Commandant wants to see you. Now.'

Mosha and Irena exchange glances. Mosha tells her, 'This isn't finished.' Irena nods as Mosha dutifully follows the Kapo out of the barrack.

The women collectively sigh. One of them mutters, 'She is mad, you know.'

Another adds, 'She's no worse than the rest of us.'

Irena listens, then interjects. 'We've all gone a little crazy here. How would you feel if you knew your sister was being forced to be a prostitute every night and it was your fault.'

The woman who shoved Mosha simply replies, 'At least her sister is still alive.'

39

Two SS soldiers stand guard outside Josef's hut. They show no reaction as the Kapo marches up with Mosha and knocks on his door. The Kapo doesn't wait; she just leaves Mosha standing there.

Josef's voice bellows from inside the hut, 'Come in!'

Mosha waits for the soldiers to open the door, but when they don't move, she pushes open the door herself and enters. She shuts the door behind her with a slam but the noise doesn't distract Josef.

He has his back to Mosha. He fiddles with his precious gramophone as Mosha just stands there, immobile. 'Für Elise', one of Beethoven's most famous – and romantic – tunes, drifts across the hut towards Mosha.

She flinches as the melody and harmonies dredge up another time, another place.

Josef slowly turns, walks over to Mosha. Walks around her, almost touches her but not quite. This time she flinches away from him, afraid of his touch, as he remarks, 'You seem to have healed well.'

Mosha says nothing, so he continues, 'How do you feel?' Still nothing from Mosha. He demands a reply, 'Answer me!'

Just one word: 'Fine.'

Josef relaxes. 'Good, good. No permanent damage?'

'No.'

Josef is dying to know, 'You can still play then?'

Mosha looks at him in disbelief. He mistakes her look for something else. 'No? You're still in pain?'

Mosha unleashes her fury. She screams in his face, 'Are you insane? I can never forgive you for what you've done to Celina. Never!'

Realising what she's done, Mosha moves away, out of his immediate reach, but Josef knows exactly how to get to her now. He calmly tells her, 'I can make it even worse for her.'

'What's worse than being raped every day?' she spits back at him.

'No one's forcing her.'

'She has no choice.'

'We all have choices. I saw you play for five hundred people with enough passion to last a lifetime. Many of them were Nazis. Yet you won't play that way for me now.'

Mosha decides to hit Josef where it hurts. 'Your mother would be ashamed of you.'

'Don't you dare…'

'What do you think she'd say if she saw you treating women like this?'

They both face off against each other as an uneasy silence fills the room. Josef breaks first.

'She was a true believer. She would understand.'

'That you order the rape of women? The shooting of men?'

Pride rises up in Josef. 'It's the true order.'

Mosha shakes her head. 'You don't really believe that.'

Josef grabs a copy of *Mein Kampf* from his desk, waves it in front of Mosha's shocked face. She tells him, 'That book is evil.'

'How dare you? You have no right to judge the *Führer*.'

Mosha just laughs in his face. And once she starts, she can't stop. This only infuriates Josef. How dare she laugh at him and his *Führer*?

Josef grabs her by the arm. 'What's so funny?'

Between her sobs of laughter, Mosha manages to get out, 'You!' which just leaves him looking confused.

The laughter finally dies down as Josef squeezes her arm, hard. Mosha tries to shake free but Josef won't release his grip on her. So she turns and faces him.

'You follow these Nazi ideals because you think it's the right thing to do, but I know you don't really believe them.'

Josef smirks. 'You know nothing.'

'But I know you. And no one who feels so passionately about music like you do could truly believe those sick, twisted ideas.'

Josef taunts her with her own words, 'But I'm a monster… remember?'

'You behave like a monster because you haven't been shown the right way. You only need to be shown the right thing to love.'

A glazed look comes over Josef's face as he begins to recite lines from *Mein Kampf*: 'Even the religion of love is only the weak reflection of the will of its exalted founder.'

He says the words almost in time to 'Für Elise', which is still softly playing in the background.

Mosha tells him, 'Stop it. Being a Nazi is the only obstacle there is to you breaking free.'

But he continues in an almost trance-like state, 'All the human culture, all the results of art, science, and technology that we see before us today, are almost exclusively the product of the Aryan.'

Mosha finally breaks free of his grasp and runs to the other side of the room. 'Stop being a Nazi and be who I truly believe you are.'

Josef blinks, comes back into the room and fixes his gaze on Mosha. He asks her, 'And who do you think I am?'

'A man who could be great.'

'I am already great.'

Tears well in Mosha's eyes. 'No. No, you're not. You're a weak puppet – who only knows how to follow orders.'

Josef grabs her again. 'The stronger must dominate and not mate with the weaker, which would signify the sacrifice of its own higher nature.'

Now she's openly crying. 'You can't even think for yourself. You could've been so different.'

Josef leans in, like a lover about to steal a kiss. 'I would've done anything for you. Orders or no orders.'

Mosha retorts, 'Except stop being a Nazi and becoming a man.' She smiles a sad smile at him.

But Josef is furious. He finally snaps and drags Mosha across the room, pushes her in front of the piano. But Mosha just stands there, so he pushes her onto the stool, then lifts the lid of the piano.

He screams at her, 'PLAY!' But Mosha just puts her hands in her lap. Again, 'PLAY! PLAY!'

Mosha reaches up slowly. Josef smiles. He thinks he's finally won. But she deliberately and gently pulls the lid down on the piano and covers the keys. She looks up at Josef and gives him a smile that would be endearing if it wasn't so smug.

Mad with rage, Josef runs over to the door and flings it open, 'Get in here!' The two SS soldiers dash inside, then stand to attention. Josef walks back over to Mosha and beckons to the soldiers. They follow him to the piano as he leans in and raises the piano lid. He takes Mosha's left hand, caresses it. For once, she doesn't try to snatch it away.

Josef gives her one last chance. 'This is your final opportunity to do the right thing.' Mosha doesn't speak to him, just shakes her head. He tightens his grip on her hand. He places her hand on the keys. They tinkle as he tries to make her play. But it quickly becomes a tug-of-war.

Josef loses his temper and slams her hand down on the keys, holding it there as Mosha struggles – and fails – to break free. With his free hand, he beckons the soldiers closer.

Following orders, they step forward. Josef now easily holds Mosha; his hand encircles her bony wrist and keeps her from moving.

He nods at the soldiers and then at Mosha. 'Hit her.'

The soldiers momentarily look confused.

'HIT HER!'

But it's not the order that's confusing them, as one of the soldiers simply asks, 'With what?'

Josef points. 'Your gun.' One of the soldiers takes his rifle from his shoulder. He hesitates, then taps the end of it across Mosha's hand. It's far too light for Josef's liking. 'Idiot!'

Josef grabs the rifle with his free handle and flips it around. WHACK. He brings the rifle butt down hard on Mosha's fingers. He smashes the butt down a second time, even harder. Mosha tries not to scream as her forefinger breaks.

But it's too much, and the sound that escapes out of her is almost musical: 'AAAAAAHHHHHHHHHHHH-HHHHHHH.'

Josef lets go of her hand with a triumphant look on his face. But Mosha just smiles up at him through the pain.

Incandescent with rage, Josef then hits Mosha in the face with the rifle butt, breaking her nose.

Blood sprays everywhere, on the piano keys and even on Josef, as Mosha slumps from the stool onto the floor. Josef stands over her as she lays there, stunned. Josef pushes her with the tip of his boot. Mosha rolls away from him.

She manages to sit up, cradling her injured hand. Somehow she defiantly stands, blood slowly still drips out of her nose, leaving a trail across the floor from the piano to where Mosha now pulls herself up to her full height. She looks Josef straight in the eye as she wipes her nose with her good hand.

She holds her broken, limp hand up in front of his face. 'You think this will change my mind? You have no idea. You could've been so great, but this just proves what a tiny little man you are.'

'Get her out of here.'

The SS soldiers each take an arm but Mosha shrugs them off and walks over to the door herself. The soldiers scramble to reach the door first and open it. Mosha reaches the door, stops and turns back to face Josef.

She holds up her good right hand – and gives him a little wave as she walks through the door, followed by the SS soldiers.

Josef watches her go, incredulity on his face.

40

Mosha bursts into the barrack. 'Irena! Irena!' Several women 'shush' her as she makes her way through the bunks, still clutching her left hand. She finds Irena lying on her bunk, trying to sleep.

Without looking up, Irena wearily asks, 'What have you done now?'

Mosha holds out her swollen hand. Irena immediately sits up, squints in the darkness. She pulls a stubby candle out from underneath her pillow, along with two precious matches. She uses one to light the candle, holds it up to Mosha's hand, sees the bent, crushed finger. 'Oy vey!'

Mosha grins at her. 'It does look worse than it feels!'

'Well, it looks pretty bad.' She moves the candle closer to Mosha. 'And so does your face.'

Irena tuts to herself as she gently takes Mosha's hand, examines it. 'It needs to be splinted. You should go to the infirmary. Your nose is broken too.'

Defiant as ever, Mosha tells her, 'No, absolutely not. I won't give him the satisfaction. You must treat it.'

Resignedly, Irena crosses over to another bunk and shakes a dark-haired woman lying there, trying to sleep. The woman tries to shake her off; she just wants to get some rest. Irena shakes her again, more forcefully. 'What?' the woman mumbles.

Irena insists, 'I need your pencil.'

The woman half laughs and tells her, 'No way.'

Irena adds, 'You'll get it back.'

The woman sits up, now a little curious. 'What do you need it for anyway?'

Irena hesitates. This could go either way. 'Mosha.'

The woman replies, 'Of course it is.'

The dark-haired woman reaches under her pillow and pulls out one of the most prized possessions in the camp – a small pencil. She looks at it for a second before she hands it over to Irena, who tells her, 'Thank you.'

Intrigued, the dark-haired woman gets off her bunk and follows Irena across to Mosha, who waits patiently on

Irena's bunk. She peers over Irena's shoulder as she takes Mosha's crooked hand. She holds up the pencil and informs her, 'This is probably going to hurt but I have to splint your finger if it's going to heal straight. I need something to bind it with.'

Mosha nods and replies, 'I still have a couple of the strips we used for my ribs.'

She quickly goes to her bunk and, with her good hand, reaches under her pillow and pulls out the strips of torn sheet, takes them back to Irena, who rips them into even smaller strips. But she takes one of the larger strips and wipes the blood from Mosha's nose.

'I think that's broken too.'

Mosha shrugs. 'I know.'

'You want me to fix that too?'

Before Mosha can even answer, Irena grabs her nose and twists it back into shape. More blood gushes out of Mosha's nostrils as tears also slip down her face, mingling to create red streaks down her cheeks to her jaw.

The candlelight flickers, giving Mosha an eerie glow as the blood drips down onto her blouse.

'Thanks?' Mosha quips.

'You're welcome,' replies Irena. 'I had to do it quick. I couldn't risk you yelling out and waking everyone.'

Irena gently takes one of the strips and wipes Mosha's face and chin clean. Then she carries on as before and places the pencil against the inside of Mosha's finger and begins to wrap the strips around it. She pulls it tighter and tighter, as Mosha winces.

Irena looks up, sees the pain in her face, but still pulls the strips tighter. Mosha nods at her, understanding that she needs to do this. Irena tells her, 'Focus on the pain in your nose, then your finger won't feel so bad!' Mosha starts to giggle but stops short when a pain shoots up her nose and across her face. She sits still and lets Irena do her work.

Irena finishes, sits back on the bunk and surveys her handiwork. 'Not the best splint I've ever done but it should work. You should be able to play again. You're lucky it's just one finger.'

Mosha holds up her hand, studies it, then looks at her other hand. 'For now.'

Irena takes Mosha's good hand. Turns it over. 'These beautiful hands, don't do anything else to ruin them.'

Mosha simply replies, 'I know what I have to do.'

'What does that mean?'

Mosha just enigmatically says, 'I'm going to give that bastard exactly what he wants.'

Irena blows out the candle.

41

March 1944

The next morning at roll call, Mosha stands in line with the other woman. Elsa is nowhere to be seen but another female leader is barking orders.

The women turn as one and prepare to leave the camp and make their way to the fields. Mosha keeps her head down but a whisper sweeps through the women. It quickly turns to a louder murmur, and someone, she's not sure who, clearly calls her name.

She looks up, looks around, but no one will make eye contact with her. As the women begin to march towards the gates, Mosha notices two soldiers tied to posts off to the side.

They have been beaten. Their faces are bruised and speckled with blood. As the women file past, Mosha sneaks a glance as them and is shocked to see they are the same SS soldiers who guarded Josef's hut the night before.

She involuntarily gasps as she makes eye contact with one of the soldiers. She mouths the words, 'I'm sorry.'

One of the soldiers looks away from Mosha, but the other one summons the last of his strength and spits at her. His phlegm hits her in the face but she makes no attempt to wipe it away. Instead, she just puts her head down and hurries past.

Today, Mosha is led away from the other women to the far end of the field, where she is all alone. She carefully picks through the rocks, looking for the one that will best suit her needs.

Two SS guard patrols walk past but they pay her no attention as they chat to each other. After they pass, Mosha picks up a smaller rock with her right hand. It fits perfectly in her palm; she cradles a fist around it. She lays her left hand out on a flat rock. Then she raises her arm and prepares to bring the rock down hard on her own hand.

At the last minute, a hand grabs her arm. She turns, shocked to find Celina standing over her. 'Stop! What are you doing?'

Mosha just sits there in disbelief. Can this be real? Is this just a mirage? Is she finally hallucinating from the malnutrition? After a couple of seconds, she jumps up and hugs Celina, clinging on for dear life, never wanting to let her go.

She forces out the words, 'Is it really you?'

Celina hugs her back. 'Yes, it's me.' The sisters stay locked in their embrace, not caring if the patrols come back.

Celina finally extricates herself from Mosha's grip. She holds her at arm's length and demands, 'What were you doing?'

Mosha ignores her – she has her own questions she needs answers to: 'How? How are you here?'

Celina quickly explains, 'I bribed an officer.' And points to one of the guards at the end of the field, the same guard who placed Mosha on her own to work.

Mosha looks at her disbelievingly. 'You didn't. I know what you had to do...'

An exasperated Celina cuts her off. 'Then why did you ask?' But Celina doesn't give her a chance to answer. 'I've only got a few minutes.'

Mosha hugs her again, notices how much thinner she is. But then, so is everyone these days. As she finally draws away, Celina notices Mosha's bandaged hand. 'What happened?'

'It's nothing.'

'Nothing?'

'Not compared to you.'

'You were about to...'

'I thought I could get through to him. I was so wrong.'

'You're finally admitting you're wrong?'

Celina smiles while Mosha breaks into a grin at the in-family joke. 'I am the only one that can play for him. But if I can't play for him at all, the threat goes away. I'll hurt him more than myself.'

The bribed SS guard patrol is heading back their way. Celina turns away so her back is to the guard and begins picking up rocks and putting them in the basket. Mosha quickly joins her. They both appear hard at work as the soldier strolls past and, without stopping, instructs them, 'You have five minutes left.'

After he passes, Celina turns to Mosha, 'I understand why you want to do it, but I don't think I can watch you.'

She reaches for Mosha's hands, holds them in her own – as she makes a startling and long buried confession: 'I hated these hands for so many years. I was so jealous of them. Of you. Of what they bought you. When we were younger, I would fantasise about damaging them, hurting you, just so you'd stop playing and I could have some of the attention for once.'

Mosha gently touches Celina's face with her bandaged hand and softly tells her, 'I know.'

Celina chokes back tears. 'You did?'

'Of course. You were such a spoiled brat about it all. You were never very good at hiding your feelings.'

'Why didn't you do anything?'

'Oh, I was just as spoiled! I thought I was far too important to be troubled with a silly little girl. Besides, Mother convinced me it was because I was so great that you were just like everyone else and wanted to be me.'

'Well, she wasn't that wrong. Actually, I wanted all the adoration and attention, I just didn't want the hard work and the hours and hours of practice.'

'And you didn't have the talent.'

Celina pretends to look offended but the sisters both burst out laughing at the same time. For the first time in years, they look at each other with real love – and respect.

Mosha speaks first: 'I can make all your dreams come true now!'

Celina realises what she is implying. 'No, absolutely not.'

'I can do one hand, but I won't be able to do the other. I need you to do that. For me.'

'No! I can't. I won't.'

But Mosha grabs the nearest rock. 'I'll do the left hand myself.' Without waiting for Celina to reply, she smashes the rock down on her own hand. Her fingers crack as the hard stone crushes them against the slab. It takes all her strength not to cry out as the tears stream down her face.

She holds the rock out to Celina, but she refuses to take it. She tries to argue, 'Your hands are everything. What if they don't heal?'

Mosha takes her hand, places the rock in it. 'I will play again one day. But right here, right now, this is the right thing to do. You know it is.'

Celina reluctantly takes it as Mosha puts her right hand down on the flat rock. Celina hesitates as Mosha tells her, 'Try to do it in one go, but if not, two or three times, until my fingers are broken. Don't stop.'

Mosha looks around, sees the guard over at the other end of the field. 'Now. Do it now.'

Celina lifts her arm, brings it down. She stops. 'I can't.'

Mosha urges her. 'You have to.'

Celina tries any way she can to get out of this. 'You can't order me around. We're not children anymore.'

'Just do it!'

Celina raises her arm again, but something is holding her back. 'I don't think I can.'

Mosha is forced to beg now. 'Please! I will never ask you for anything ever again.'

Celina smiles. 'Liar!'

Mosha tells her, 'This is what I want. This will stop this silly game he insists on playing. This will save us.'

'But what if it doesn't? What if it...'

Mosha urges her, 'It won't. I know him.'

Something in Mosha's voice this time convinces Celina, who raises her arms in the air once more. But before she can bring it down, a hand grabs her arm. KLEIN!

The sisters had been so focused on each other, neither of them had heard Elsa approaching. She looks from Celina to Mosha. 'What are you doing?'

Celina instantly drops the rock at their feet as Mosha steps forward. 'What I should've done months ago.'

A sneering Elsa tells her, 'You'll never win.'

Mosha is so tired of this game. Tired of Elsa. Tired of bowing down to someone who hates her, her faith and everything about her. Suddenly, Mosha doesn't care what happens to her, she just wants to be left alone.

She squares off against the female guard, looks her in the eye and without fear, asks her, 'What do you care? I know I'm in your way. If I do this, he won't care about me anymore. You will have won.'

Elsa knows the paradigm has shifted. She looks uneasily at Mosha. 'I don't know what you mean.' She tries to sound authoritative but her voice comes out as a squeak.

Mosha knows she's got the upper hand. 'Just let me do it. Walk away. Pretend you never saw me. This is all on me.'

Elsa is about to acquiesce when Celina shakes her head. 'I can't.'

Without looking at her sister and keeping her eyes firmly fixed on Elsa, Mosha says, 'Yes, you can. You will do this.'

Elsa smirks, 'Now who's the monster?'

Mosha picks up the rock and holds it out to Elsa. 'Then why don't you do it?'

Elsa greedily grabs the rock from her. Tosses it up in the air and catches it, almost like a ball. Mosha once again puts her hand out flat on the big rock. Celina moves next to her, puts her arm around her, but can't look.

Without hesitation, Elsa raises her arm. Brings down the rock. Once. Twice. She makes sure she smashes all of Mosha's fingers, not just one or two. Elsa then carelessly tosses the rock to one side. She looks at the sisters. Tears run down Celina's face, while Mosha shows no emotion at all.

Now it's Mosha's turn to comfort Celina. 'Don't waste your tears.'

She then turns to Elsa. 'Thank you.'

Elsa laughs before saying, 'I didn't do it for you.'

Mosha replies, 'I know, but thank you anyway.'

Elsa is not sure how to respond to that, so instead she turns to Celina, back in guard mode, and barks the order, 'Get back to the factory.'

Mosha nods at Celina. 'It's okay. I'm going to be fine.'

A heartbroken Celina takes one last look at Mosha's battered and broken hands. This may have been her silly, childish dream all those years ago but now she can't stop sobbing as she walks away.

42

Josef sits at his desk in his cosy little cottage. He turns on a Volksempfänger radio and settles back to listen to a radio broadcast by the Reich Broadcasting Corporation.

Adolf Hitler's voice blares out: 'The Reich is being supported in this by the allied nations, which from Europe to East Asia are also determined to defend the substance of their blood and the values of their cultures. Above all, it has comrades in arms in those nations which realise that their own future is possible...'

Josef mouths along to the words. He knows this speech off by heart, as the radio has been playing it over and over again all week. He reaches out, fiddles with the dial, and a BBC Worldwide report replaces Hitler. Without realising he is doing it, Josef guiltily looks around. He could get into a lot of trouble for listening to the BBC report, but he's the only one in his home. Still, he turns the volume dial down, just in case.

The voice on the radio says: 'Here is a special bulletin. Early this morning, the long-awaited British and American invasion began when paratroops landed in the area of the Somme estuary. The harbour of Le Havre is being fiercely bombarded at the present moment. Naval forces of the German Navy are off the coast, fighting with enemy landing vessels. This is the latest news from Berlin.'

Josef turns the dial on the radio to *Off*, picks up the phone and dials a number. 'Yes. This is SS-*Gruppenführer* Hanke. I need to speak to SS-*Oberst-Gruppenführer* Helldorf. Yes, of course.'

A few seconds pass before Josef speaks again. 'Yes, sir. I don't think we should move the prisoners right now. The march to Auschwitz will attract too much attention.'

On the other end of the line, Helldorf agrees. 'Yes. I've already discussed this with the *Führer*. We will move them once we know what's happening with the invasion.'

Josef asks, 'So should we still prepare?'

Helldorf replies, 'Always be ready.'

The line goes dead. Josef hangs up and turns the radio back up. 'Again, the reports from Berlin say there is heavy fighting between the Germans and the Allied forces on the Normandy peninsula. From Cherbourg to Le Havre, from the sea to the air...'

There's a knock on the door, so Josef quickly turns the radio off. 'Come in.'

A young SS officer enters. He waits, as is the custom, to be addressed first. A slightly irritated Josef says, 'Yes?'

The officer is nervous and clears his throat before answering, 'I thought you should know…'

'What? Know what?'

The officer seems more embarrassed than anything. He clearly wishes he were anywhere but here.

He takes a deep breath. 'Mosha Gebert is in the infirmary.'

Josef quickly rises from his chair, startling the young officer, who stumbles back a step.

'Why?'

The officer looks down at the floor and mumbles, 'Her hands.'

Josef corrects him. 'You mean her finger?'

But the officer replies, 'No, sir. Both her hands. They've been smashed.'

Josef pushes past the officer and rushes out. Minutes later he stands in front of the infirmary doors. Something holds him back. For a split second he's afraid of what he'll find if he enters.

Inside, Mosha is set on the edge of a chair just inside the door. Elsa and a Kapo stand next to her like sentry guards.

Moans echo throughout the building as dozens of patients are laid out on bare bunk beds, many writhing in pain from both their injuries and the primitive conditions. There are no blankets and the hard headrests are filled with sawdust and straw.

Ill-equipped nurses – called *kalifaktors* – wander up and down the room, peering at the injured and sick but not really doing anything for them. Most of the patients have come here to die and they know it. If the malnutrition, hunger and beatings don't get them, then the typhoid fever will.

There's a reason Mosha wanted to stay away – she's afraid once you walk into this building, there's no getting out. The women – and men – who enter the infirmary are rarely treated or saved and usually just get sicker and sicker.

Elsa nudges the Kapo. 'Wrap her hands.'

But Mosha moves them out of the way – she can't bear anyone to touch them. She implores, 'Just leave them.'

The Kapo grabs some bandages, moves towards Mosha as Josef bursts through the door. He demands, 'What the hell happened?'

Elsa grabs one of Mosha's hands, holds it up for him to see. Mosha snatches her hand back, looks away. Elsa insists, 'Tell him.'

Defiantly, Mosha says, 'I did it. I broke my hands.'

Instead of getting mad at Mosha, Josef angrily turns to Elsa. 'Why didn't you stop her?'

Elsa sees how angry he is and realises she can never admit she was the one who wielded the rock. Instead, she brazens it out. 'This is not my fault.'

'You should've stopped her.' Josef slaps Elsa hard across the face. She is stunned. He goes to strike her again but she quickly steps back, just out of reach.

Mosha jumps up and stands between them. 'Stop it. I did this. I did it to myself. She is not to blame.'

Josef grabs her shoulders and shakes her. 'You're a liar. There's no way you did this to both your hands. You didn't do it alone.'

When Mosha refuses to name her accomplice, Josef shouts, 'Who did this?'

She stubbornly insists, 'It was me. Only me.'

Elsa seizes her chance. 'It was her sister.'

The two women exchange a look of hatred but Mosha knows anything she says now will only make it worse for Celina. Elsa will make her life even more of a living hell than it already is.

Josef directs his question at Elsa: 'Where is that whore Celina now?'

Elsa eagerly tells him, 'I sent her back to her little pleasure room, where she belongs.'

Josef looks Mosha in the eye. 'She will be punished for this.'

'It's not her fault. If you want to punish anyone, punish me.'

Josef tenderly takes Mosha's broken hands in his. 'Why?'

Mosha looks directly into his eyes. 'It's easier this way.' She then snatches her hands back.

Josef takes a step back away from her as a cold look passes over his face. 'Then you are of no use to me.'

Elsa smirks as Mosha gives a sigh of relief. She feels a huge weight lift from her shoulders. She's close to tears but won't give it up. Elsa steps forward, gently touches Josef's arm. 'What do you want me to do with her? She can't play the piano, and she certainly can't work in the fields now.'

Josef tells Elsa, 'Make sure her hands heal.'

Elsa can't believe what she is hearing, 'No punishment? Nothing?'

Now it's Josef's turn to smirk. 'Get her and her silly little choir ready for Auschwitz. They march at the end of July.'

Elsa finally looks happy, 'Of course.'

She grabs Mosha by the arm and pulls her back down into the seat, nods at the Kapo to finally begin the bandaging of the hands.

But Josef isn't finished yet; he instructs Elsa, 'And take her sister off the factory work duty and put her to work with the *Sonderkommando*, when she's not needed to service the soldiers.'

Josef steps right up to Mosha, leans down so their faces are almost touching. He sneers at her, 'Nothing to say?'

Mosha very calmly replies, 'I joyfully hasten to meet death. If it comes before I have had opportunity to develop all my artistic faculties, it will come, my hard fate notwithstanding, too soon, and I should probably wish it later – yet even then I shall be happy, for will it not deliver me from a state of endless suffering?'

Josef just looks bemused. 'Quoting Beethoven won't help you or your sister now.' They just look at each other, neither of them willing to give an inch.

Elsa has no idea what's going on between the two of them but she wants to be far away from their mind games. 'And her?' She points at Mosha as Josef decides her fate.

'Put her in the arrival area for now. We have new *häftlings* coming from Trawniki. She can count them in and out. And let me know the minute her hands have healed.'

Josef turns, strides out of the infirmary as the Kapo places the last of the bandages around Mosha's hands. She just sits and waits for Elsa to make her next move – and she doesn't disappoint. She grabs Mosha by her upper arm, pulls her out of the seat and shoves her away from the death and the disease here and into something much, much worse.

43

Several days later, the snow is finally melting in the late spring sun. Male prisoners are sorting through yet more bodies in more execution pits. They struggle to move them into a pile in a large pit behind the crematorium. They struggle because of the smell but also because they are so weak and can hardly stand themselves. This is backbreaking work and they are so ill-fed, but they have no choice – move the pile or be on the pile.

The stench of piss and human faeces fills the air but the men hardly seem to notice. Some are lucky enough to have a tattered or threadbare scarf wrapped around their faces in a poor attempt to block it out, but others are not so lucky. But lately they've been removing so many hundreds and hundreds of bodies out of the pits and into the crematorium to be burned that they've become immune, completely desensitised to the stink that wafts all around them.

One person who still isn't used to this is Celina. She stands by the pile of bodies, gagging and trying not to throw up. It's her fifth day with this crew, a lone woman in a job usually reserved for the men. She's the first woman to be forced to do this work – the crew know she's being punished for something very bad but she refuses to speak to them. Instead, she keeps her head down and tries to stifle her gags. She will never get the smell of death out of her clothes or her hair.

As the men throw the latest bodies on the pile, it's Celina's job to remove any gold teeth or fillings from the victims before they are burned in the crematorium. It's a horrific job, but it's her punishment. She knows this. And while every tooth she pulls makes her physically sick and leaves the soldiers pointing and laughing at her, she knows it could be worse. She could be lying on the pile.

After any gold teeth are removed, Celina places them in a container near her feet. A container that is filling up more quickly than she thought possible. She wonders how the prisoners can have so many gold fillings, dental caps and dentures to be extracted for melting down into gold bars for the Nazis to hoard.

But when she looks at the bodies piling up, she quickly realises it's not that the prisoners each have so much gold in their mouths – it's the sheer volume of prisoners being murdered. Celina holds back several sobs as it dawns on her exactly how many Jews – both men and women – are being slaughtered.

As she works her way through the pile, the bodies are removed by a different crew and taken over to the crematorium to be burned. But the pile never seems to diminish.

As two of the men drop another body near Celina's feet, one of them leans in and nudges her. She snaps out of her trance and sees a soldier stalking towards her. She smiles thanks at the man but he just ignores her and heads back into the gas chamber. Celina coughs several times, takes a deep breath, leans down to the body and checks his mouth.

While Celina is mining for gold in dead prisoners' mouths, Mosha is logging in the new prisoners that have been shipped to the camp, now that there's finally space for them.

As the prisoners are loaded off the trucks, they approach the area where Mosha sits at a table next to a stern-looking Block Elder. She counts the prisoners as they file past. Her hands are still bent and misshapen, a couple of fingers are still splinted, but she manages to hold a pencil in her left hand.

As each *häftling* files past, she makes a clumsy mark on the paper in front of her. Luckily, the Block Elder writes down their names, while Mosha just has to mark if they are male or female and if they are children.

The stubby pencil falls out of her crooked hand, rolls along the table and falls to the floor. Mosha scrambles to pick it up as the Block Elder glares at her. It's not the first time she's dropped the pencil today. She apologises but the woman doesn't have time for this. She tells Mosha, 'Keep up.'

Mosha looks up at the never-ending line of prisoners, carries on making the check marks on her paper.

Later that night, Mosha sits on her bunk. She's exhausted. Even just sitting down marking a piece of paper has left her drained, both mentally and physically. Working in the fields is hard on the body, but seeing all the new prisoners arrive has overwhelmed her.

She carefully unwraps her hands and removes the splints. She tries to stretch out her fingers, flex them in and out, but it's tough. She tries to play imaginary piano scales, but her fingers hardly move and several are still bent at odd angles. Still, she closes her eyes, lost in the sound in her head.

'Mosha!'

She opens her eyes. Irena is standing next to her bunk, an excited look on her face.

'Have you heard?'

Mosha replies wearily, 'Heard what?'

'We're leaving.'

Mosha can't look Irena in the eye. She knows this already. But she forces herself to ask, 'When?'

Irena sits down on the end of the bunk. 'Soon. Lotte overheard some of the guards talking about how they had to get us ready.'

But there are some things Mosha doesn't know. 'Did they say where?'

Irena shrugs. 'Probably another camp.'

Mosha knows she has to say something. 'Don't get your hopes up. They're not called death marches for nothing.'

Irena admits, 'I know. I just have to believe we're going to some place better. Nowhere can be as bad as here.'

'Can't it? You've heard new prisoners talking about where they've comes from. Everywhere is hell.'

'I know. But there's always hope.'

Mosha just closes her eyes again as Irena heads back to her own bunk. The only place Mosha wants to be is lost in the music swirling around in her head.

44

Several weeks later, the women stand in the crisp early summer air for roll call. There's a chill in the dawn air but the sun is struggling to break through. Elsa stands on the platform in front of all the women.

She steps down and begins to walk among them, looking them over, making them nervous. An inspection like this is never good news. Elsa stops abruptly in font of Mosha. 'Show me your hands.'

Mosha holds out her still-bandaged hands. Elsa turns them over. 'Take off the bandages.' Mosha does as she's told but Elsa looks far from pleased. She stalks back to the platform. A Kapo nods at her. Elsa, in turn, nods to an SS officer. The siren sounds and the women file out as the workday begins.

Elsa leaves the field and makes her way over to Josef's house. She is tired of having to report to him every morning after inspecting Mosha's hands. But orders are orders, and she wants to impress him.

She stands outside the house, waiting to be summoned. Josef calls out, 'Enter.' She walks in and stands in front of his desk, waiting.

Josef looks at her. 'Well?'

He's not happy when Elsa tells him, 'Not yet.'

Exasperated, he wants to know, 'How much longer will it take?'

Elsa reminds him, 'I'm not a doctor. But they are almost healed, so I would guess just a few more days.'

Josef nods. 'Good. *SS-Oberst-Gruppenführer* Helldorf wants to move the remaining women next week.'

Elsa is surprised. 'So soon?'

'He wants everyone moved in the next few weeks.'

'Is everyone going?'

'Everyone. We will move the prisoners in small groups – they will be easier to control on the marches.'

'Where are they going?'

'They will be sent to various other camps, including Natzweiler, Gross-Rosen, Auschwitz, Płaszów, Ravensbrück and Mauthausen. Once the men have gone, most of the women will go. The choir will be last to leave.'

'And me?'

'You will be moved with the last of the women. A handful of male prisoners will stay for now and continue working. We can only march so many at a time. But we will need to reduce the number of men before we move them.'

'Will you be going too?'

'When the last of the men are moved. They want as many prisoners as possible moved before the end of July. So the first men will leave in the morning.'

Elsa seductively inches towards Josef, leans across the desk, but he flinches. 'Josef… I…'

He cuts her off. 'Don't.'

But Elsa believes this may now be her only chance to show her true feelings. 'But we could…'

'I don't feel that way.'

Elsa can't help herself and snaps, 'Why are you still so fascinated with her?'

Josef knows he doesn't have to explain himself to anyone, let alone an inferior officer, but even now he can't help but defend Mosha. 'To see and hear her play, it's like I'm listening to…'

'To what?'

Josef stands up, faces Elsa. 'Never mind, you won't ever understand. How could you?'

She's offended, but that doesn't deter her. 'Then help me to understand.' She reaches out for him again.

'NO!' Josef steps out of her reach, but it's the look on his face that makes Elsa back away. 'Bring her to me tomorrow.'

'No. I won't do it.'

'You would defy me?'

In a pleading voice, Elsa finally decides to take a chance to open up and reveal her true feelings. It's now or never. 'She doesn't deserve you. She doesn't love you. But I do.'

Quick as a flash, Josef is around the desk, grabbing Elsa by the throat. 'You will do as I order or you will face the consequences. Do you understand?' Elsa tries to nod but Josef squeezes tighter. 'Do you?'

He lets go. Elsa splutters, backs away, real fear in her eyes. She squeaks out, 'Yes.'

His temper once again in check, Josef acts as though nothing just happened and calmly tells her, 'You are dismissed.'

Elsa pulls herself together, gives him one last look and leaves, holding her throat. Josef crosses to the gramophone, selects a record, puts on Beethoven's *Egmont* and sits back at his desk. The photo of his mother is in pride of place, staring back at him. He grabs the frame, clasps it to his chest, closes his eyes, lost in the music.

45

July 24, 1944

Dawn. With just the choir and a handful of political prisoners left in the camp, there's no roll call.

But the women still rise, get ready for the day. Mosha checks her hands, re-bandages them with the help of Irena. They have just finished wrapping the last strip when Elsa walks through the barracks.

She stops directly in front of Mosha. 'He wants to see you.'

Mosha looks at her. The collar of her uniform is pulled up but the bruising around her neck is still visible. Mosha tries to get a better look but Elsa turns away too quickly. Irena raises her eyebrows at Mosha but they say nothing.

Mosha follows Elsa out of the barrack. By now, the women are used to Mosha being pulled out, but today something feels different. Many of them stop what they are doing to watch Mosha leave. Lotte runs over to Irena. 'What's happening?'

Irena has to admit, 'I don't know.'

Lotte is worried. 'Will Mosha be all right?'

Irena gives the young girl a reassuring smile, even though deep down she's frightened herself. 'Yes, I am sure she will be. You know Mosha. That girl has more lives than a cat!'

Irena shoos Lotte back to her bunk. 'You'd better get ready.' Lotte smiles back at her. As she heads back over to her own bunk, Irena bows her head and says a prayer, '*SheElohim yevarach otha*' (God bless you).

Across the camp, Mosha enters Josef's little house. She's surprised to see Celina already standing in front of Josef's desk.

Celina is beyond skinny, and she's tired and on the verge of collapse, but she lights up when Mosha enters the room.

The sisters rush into each other's arms and embrace as Josef watches from behind his desk.

He watches them, lets them have their little moment, before dropping his bombshell: 'I am glad you are happy to see each other. Celina will leave tomorrow with the other women for Auschwitz.'

Celina breaks away from her sister. 'You bastard.'

Mosha simply asks, 'And me?'

'You will stay here. With me.'

'I'd rather go on the death march to Auschwitz.'

Josef laughs. 'But it's not your choice, is it?'

Now Mosha laughs. 'You still haven't won. I won't play.'

'I'm not keeping you around to play.'

'Why can't you just let me go?' Mosha walks around the desk. Stands in front of Josef. She's a shell of the woman who walked into the camp a year ago. She barely weighs a hundred pounds, her cheekbones are sunken, her once silky hair is now thin and flat, and her hands are a twisted mess.

But in his eyes, she's still the most beautiful woman in the world.

He speaks softly. 'You will never belong to anyone but me.'

Mosha replies, 'I don't belong to anyone. None of us do. You can starve us, torture us, imprison us in this wretched camp. But our minds and souls are free.'

She walks over to Celina. The sisters stand side by side in solidarity. Celina looks him in the eye, then at Mosha. 'I'm ready to die.'

Mosha replies, 'Don't say that. No one is dying today.'

Celina turns to look at Josef. 'You think that by torturing us to punish Mosha, you won. But it just means we didn't die. You could've had us killed but you didn't because you were so consumed with having power over her.'

She takes a step closer to him and hits home with the truth. 'Mosha is the reason we're still alive. She saved us.'

Josef jumps out of his chair and grabs Mosha, pulls her towards him; almost in a lover's embrace, he holds her from behind. He pulls his pistol from the holster and holds the gun up by Mosha's ear again.

But then he points it at Celina. 'Not anymore.'

He fires the gun. BANG! The bullet hits Celina in the chest and she drops to the floor. Blood seeps out from underneath her.

Mosha is momentarily confused. Everything seems to be unfolding in slow motion as she sees Celina fall to the ground. Mosha pushes Josef away and as he loosens his grip on her, she drops to her knees.

Tears are streaming down her face but she doesn't even know that she's crying. She shakes Celina, again and again, but there's no response. She cradles Celina in her arms, blood soaking into her own thin, raggedy clothes.

Mosha screams, 'Celina! Celina!'

Celina opens her eyes but it takes her a few seconds to focus on Mosha. Her lips move but Mosha can't hear her. The gunshot has momentarily deafened her once again.

Celina whispers, 'I'm sorry. I love you.'

Between sobs, Mosha manages to tell her back, 'I love you too.' Mosha hugs her close for several seconds, but as she releases her, Celina's eyes close, her body goes limp. Mosha lays her gently on the floor and then lies across her, not wanting to ever let go, even as Celina's blood soaks into her clothing, turning her drab grey outfit into a tide of red.

But Josef has other ideas. He grabs Mosha by her shoulders and pulls her to her feet. He's talking to her; his lips are moving but she can't hear what he's saying. She's paralysed to the spot, her eyes never leaving Celina's lifeless body. Now Josef is yelling, but still nothing registers with her. He grabs her chin and forces her to look at him. The action jolts Mosha back to the present.

She turns and beats Josef's chest with her crippled fists. It's ineffective and he lets her wail on him for a few seconds before he easily grabs her hands to stop the weak pummelling. With just one of his hands around her small, bony wrists, he drags her away from Celina and over to the desk, the gun still in his other hand.

They grapple as he tries to push her body down onto the desk. Josef easily has a hundred pounds of muscle on her but Mosha is determined to fight to the end. His strong hold on her wrists only makes her try even harder. She manages to get a hand free and lashes out, barely hitting him in the face.

He swears at her, '*Verdammt*,' just as Mosha's hand connects with something on the desk. She grabs the photo frame of Josef's mother on the desk. She smashes it hard into the side of his face.

The corner of the frame opens a gash just above his eyebrow. Blood drips from the cut onto her face, into her mouth.

She can taste the blood – his blood – and it only fuels her determination. She slams the frame into his head a second time, but now it just glances off him as he moves his head backwards, away from her.

Mosha's efforts only fuel Josef's anger. He spies his *SS-Ehrendegen* (Honour Sword) leaning against the wall just a few feet away. He throws the gun across the room and struggles to hold Mosha still while reaching for the long, thin blade.

His hand grasps the black ribbed wooden grip, which is bound with silver wire and features an inset disc featuring the SS lightning bolt runes. He pulls the sword out of its black-painted scabbard. He doesn't have time to admire the hours that have gone into creating this fine weapon that was awarded to him with a hand-signed certificate from Heinrich Himmler.

But he's used it before. He knows it will slice through the hardest of materials. Even bone. He briefly lets go of both of Mosha's hands, then grabs the left one and slams it down on the desk with the words, 'We're going to make a little concerto of our own.'

Somehow during their tussle, he manages to pull her sleeve up, exposing her wrist and arm. He places the sword across her wrist. He runs it back and forth, not hard enough to cut deeply but just enough to draw a little blood.

Mosha suddenly stops struggling. She looks over at Celina's lifeless body. She finally – and calmly – accepts her fate. She doesn't care anymore. She mouths the words, 'Ever thine, ever mine, ever ours.'

Josef is so caught up in his rage he doesn't hear her, and for a moment doesn't realise she's no longer fighting him. He triumphantly asks her, 'Will you be able to hear your own screams?'

Mosha doesn't reply. She just smiles a sad, knowing smile. She places her right hand around Josef's hand that grips the sword. She keeps it there as he raises the sword high above both their heads.

Mosha closes her eyes and braces herself. BANG!

46

She doesn't hear the gunfire but she feels wetness spray across her hand and then Josef as he slumps forward, almost knocking her over.

Mosha opens her eyes as a Russian soldier bursts into the room with his gun drawn. He says something to her, but her hearing is still muted. His lips move again, she tries to read them. She thinks he's saying, 'Are you okay?' but she's not sure. She points to her ear and shakes her head.

She turns, crouches by Celina's body. Her broken, bloody hand caresses her sister's face. She leans over, kisses her cold lips. The soldier gently touches Mosha's shoulder. She stands, looks over at Josef.

He's still slumped across the desk, but alive. He clutches his shoulder in pain. The bullet hit him just below the collarbone. He's losing blood but he's still conscious. The soldier approaches him, gun pointed. Josef straightens up and laughs in the soldier's face.

Two more Russian soldiers enter the room. They each grab one of Josef's arms. He winces from the pain but his laughter becomes maniacal. The soldiers drag him towards the door. Before they can get him outside, he breaks free of their grip and turns to face Mosha.

'You'll never forget me now.' The soldiers reach for him again but he shrugs them off and walks out of the door on his own.

The first soldier looks sadly at Celina's body and then at Mosha. He's been shocked by what the soldiers have found in the camp – dozens of battered and broken people. But the sight of Mosha covered in her sister's blood leaves him close to tears.

Mosha is rooted to the spot; she doesn't know what to do. Why are these soldiers here? It takes a few minutes for her mind to decipher what's happening. She looks lost as the soldier gently takes her by the arm and steers her out of the house.

Loud sirens suddenly sound across the camp, making Mosha jump. She looks up just as an Allied plane swoops out of nowhere and heads towards the open fields beyond the camp. The siren sounds again and Mosha looks around into chaos as both SS soldiers and the few prisoners that are left run in all directions.

Explosions can be heard in the distance as Russian soldiers swarm the camp. They round up the few remaining SS soldiers who don't fight back. They know it's over. There are less than five hundred male prisoners left in the camp and just the women from the choir. The soldiers also begin escorting them out of the barracks and into the main field. They look just as confused and scared as Mosha. At first, they don't understand what is happening – until they see the SS soldiers on their knees with Russian guns trained at their heads.

Some of the braver prisoners – both men and women – walk over to the SS soldiers and spit on them, just like the soldiers had done to them over and over again.

'Scum.'

'Utter filth.'

'Nazi scum.'

The Russian soldiers just stand, watch and don't try to stop the women, even when one of them picks up a pebble nearby and hurls it at one of the soldiers' heads.

The soldiers direct Josef over to the post by the gates. He stumbles before he reaches it. He's getting weaker from the blood loss but he's determined not to show any vulnerability now. He holds his head high as they tie him to the post, and then stand guard either side of him. Mosha has followed them into the compound in a daze and now stands just inside the gates, just feet away from where Josef hangs, taking it all in.

She doesn't dare believe that she's finally free – that, after all this time, the camp is being liberated. But she knows deep down she will never be free of this place. It will always be with her.

There's a commotion on the other side of the field as the Russian soldiers appear to be fighting someone. As the soldiers move, Mosha sees Elsa being half dragged across the compound – and she's putting up one hell of a fight. She repeatedly punches Russian soldiers and it takes three of them to subdue her. They finally hit her in the face with a rifle butt, force her to her knees and tie her hands behind her back. She looks up, sees Mosha watching everything. Their eyes meet. If looks could kill, Mosha would be dead right now.

Outside the gates, furniture from Josef's little house flies out the door. It lands in a heap on the road that leads into the camp. Chairs, books, lamps. Several gramophone records hit the gravel. The bloodied photo of Josef and his mother hits the top of the pile.

A Russian *Komdiv* (Division Commander) walks out of the house, surveys the pile, kicks over a few things in his disgust. Four Russian soldiers carry Josef's piano out of the door. They stand it next to the pile of discarded furniture.

The *Komdiv* instructs them, 'Burn it. Burn it all.'

He looks over to the compound in the distance and sees someone tied to the post. 'No, wait.' The soldiers stand back from the pile and wait for further instructions. The *Komdiv* asks one of them, 'Is that Commandant Hanke?'

'I believe so, sir.'

'Get that piano, the gramophone and records and follow me.'

The *Komdiv* strides across the short stretch past the SS sector to the compound gates. The soldiers struggle to keep up as three of them hoist the piano and half carry, half drag it after him, while the fourth soldier grabs the broken gramophone and a couple of the records. As they reach the post where Josef is now slumped, the *Komdiv* gestures them to place everything just a few feet away from him.

'Now burn it.'

47

Mosha didn't hear the *Komdiv*'s instructions, but she knows they are about to destroy the piano and rushes forward. She waves her hands at the soldiers. They stop, look at her. She reaches out and tentatively touches the piano of her own free will. Josef watches, fascinated, as her fingers run over the keys. The soldiers look over at the *Komdiv*. He shrugs as Mosha yells, 'Not the piano.'

Irena appears out of nowhere and grabs her arm. 'Are you mad? After all the pain, you want to save his piano?'

Mosha closes her eyes. Irena shakes her until she opens them again. Irena gestures at the piano. She stands right in front of Mosha. 'Why?'

She looks at the piano and then back at Irena. Still a little deaf in her ear, she raises her voice. 'I can't bear to see something so beautiful destroyed. It's not the piano's fault.'

Irena understands. She walks over to the *Komdiv*. 'Please don't destroy it. Not yet.'

The *Komdiv* is watching Mosha closely as once again she runs her hands up and down the keys. He nods at Irena, who takes a chance.

'Can you get a chair?'

The *Komdiv* momentarily looks perplexed but then realises why Irena wants it and nods at one of his soldiers. The soldier runs off back towards the house and returns moments later with the stool in his arms. He hands it over to Irena, who takes it over to where Mosha is still delicately caressing the piano.

She puts the stool down on the ground behind Mosha, then taps her on the shoulder. Mosha turns, looks at Irena, who gestures at the stool. Mosha is overcome with emotion, and tears streak down her face. Irena, in turn, also starts to cry, and the women fall into each other's arms. They cling together for several seconds before Irena pulls away and wipes the tears from Mosha's face.

Mosha looks at the piano. She sits down, unsure if she should do this. She looks at her hands, holds them out, flexes them several times, tries to stretch them out. She tries a few notes as she dips her head close to the keys, but realises that, to her, it sounds as disjointed as her fingers.

She practises a couple of scales, just like the imaginary ones she's been doing for months. Slowly, she tries a couple of Chopin's Preludes to get her once elegant fingers to move. She gives up. She lays the left side of her head on the keys in disappointment, not caring there is blood smeared across them, just wanting to be close to the music somehow. She keeps tapping the keys with her right hand, and soon she can hear a faint noise. She smiles to herself. Irena taps her shoulder again and Mosha lifts her head off the piano, looks up at her. She tries a couple of notes again.

Irena bends down so her lips are close to Mosha's ear. She whispers so only Mosha can hear, 'Play us to freedom.'

Mosha looks over at Josef. His head is now slumped on his chest and she can't tell if he's alive or dead. But she doesn't care anymore. She looks up at Irena and mouths the word, 'Freedom.'

Mosha begins to play – Beethoven's 'Ode to Joy'.

At first, she sounds like a five-year-old. Plunk. Plunk. Plunk. She stops, makes a half fist, then flexes her hands, composes herself, starts again.

This time, the music sounds right. It gradually gets louder and louder and soon soars above the noise of the soldiers and prisoners who run through the camp. The beautiful, haunting sound stops everyone in their tracks. The soldiers stop to listen, the prisoners stop to listen. Even the Russian *Komdiv*, who has strict guidelines to follow, stops barking orders and leans in closer.

Irena squeezes Mosha's shoulder in reassurance and looks up to see the crowd begin to gather. Lotte and what's left of the women's choir push their way through the crowd to the front. Lotte exclaims, 'It's Mosha!'

The women hug each other and several begin to cry. Then the women all join hands and stand together in a line. Josef's eyes flutter open. He raises his head, looks at Mosha as he strains to hear. He has the same look now as he did fourteen years ago when he saw her play in Berlin. He's transfixed.

But Mosha is oblivious to Josef or anyone else behind her. Like she was in Berlin, she's lost in the music, in the moment. She could be back on the stage instead of seated at a rickety old piano in a muddy field. Her hands spring back to life once more as they dart across the keys. There are more than a few missteps, a few wrong notes as Mosha's broken fingers struggle to find the rhythm. But suddenly, she is playing as she used to before.

The music gets louder, more intense, more passionate.

One lone voice from the back of the crowd sings a verse:

Joy, beautiful spark of the gods,
Daughter from Elysium,
We enter, drunk with fire.

Another voice joins in, then another. The women from the choir take over. They turn to face the other soldiers and prisoners. This is the moment they've been practising for. They just didn't know it. Their voices ring out, crisp and clear across the compound:

Heavenly One, thy sanctuary!
Your magic joins again
What convention strictly divides.

Lotte and most of the women are now singing through their tears:

All people become brothers,
Where your gentle wing abides.

More and more voices join in. Men, women, prisoners, even some of the Russian soldiers:

All creatures drink of joy
At nature's breast.

Just and unjust
Alike taste of her gift;
She gave us kisses and the fruit of the vine.

Mosha is in her own world. Her eyes are closed and she's completely lost in the music as tears stream down her face. She's halfway through the piece and most of the camp has stopped to hear her play. The crowd grows larger with each note.

The only sounds across the camp are the piano and the choir. Everything else has stopped. No gunfire, no shouts, no explosions. The voices grow stronger, in harmony, together:

All creatures drink of joy
At nature's breast.
Just and unjust
Alike taste of her gift;
She gave us kisses and the fruit of the vine,
A tried friend to the end.
Even the worm has been granted sensuality,
And the cherub stands before God!
Gladly, as His heavenly bodies fly.

Several of the prisoners have fallen to the ground. They sob as they lie on the ground. But these are tears of pure joy. Mosha continues to play, completely unaware of what is happening behind her. The voices continue:

On their courses through the heavens,
Thus, brothers, you should run your race,
As a hero going to conquest.

You millions, I embrace you.
This kiss is for all the world!
Brothers, above the starry canopy
There must dwell a loving Father.
Do you fall in worship, you millions?
World, do you know your creator?
Seek him in the heavens;
Above the stars must He dwell.

Mosha's eyes are still closed as she reaches the crescendo. Then silence. The only sound in the camp now is from both prisoners' and soldiers' sobs.

Irena leans in and hugs her. She slowly pulls Mosha to her feet, gently turns her around to face the crowd gathered behind her. Irena leans right in to her left ear. 'Open your eyes.'

Mosha opens her eyes. Sees the prisoners standing as one; every single one of them has their hands over their hearts. Tears stream down her face as she scans the crowd.

Her eyes catch Elsa, still on her knees, with the other Nazi prisoner soldiers. Their eyes meet as Elsa is pulled to her feet and marched away towards the gates. She turns back, looks at Mosha. She gives the Jewish girl a curt nod. Finally respect.

Mosha looks directly at Josef, tears streaming down his face. He openly sobs as Mosha walks towards him. She stops directly in front of him. The Russian *Komdiv* walks over, nods at the soldiers, who raise their guns at Josef. But Mosha reaches out, pushes the guns down, away from him. She looks up; their eyes lock.

She says just two simple words: 'Thank you.'

Then Mosha turns, walks away, joins the other female prisoners, their arms entwined around each other as they walk through the camp gates. Behind her, gunfire echoes across the field.

Mosha wipes away the tears and doesn't look back. She keeps walking. To freedom.

HISTORY OF MAJDANEK

Auschwitz is probably the best-known concentration camp that was operated by the Nazis during World War II. But Majdanek was one of the largest camps in operation – and is notorious for the single most executions, when 18,400 prisoners were murdered in just one day.

The camp was initially called Kriegsgefangenenlager der Waffen SS Lublin, and in February 1943 was renamed Konzentrationslager Lublin. But it got its nickname Majdanek – which means 'Little Majdan' – in 1941 by local residents, as it was adjacent to the Lublin ghetto of Majdan Tatarski. And the name stuck.

Construction of the camp began in 1941 on the order of Heinrich Himmler. Visiting Lublin in July 1941, Himmler entrusted Odilo Globocnik, the SS and police commander in the Lublin district, with building a camp 'for 25,000 to 50,000 inmates who would be used to work in SS and police workshops and at construction sites'.

The initial plans for the camp indicated it was to hold 150,000 prisoners and prisoners of war at any one time, but it was vastly downsized as building supplies became scarce during the war.

The camp was intended to be the source of a free workforce for the Third Reich's expansion in the East, but that ideal didn't last long and soon Majdanek became a killing ground.

In the three years the camp operated – from 1941 through to 1944 – it expanded to include two gas chambers, crematoriums, wooden gallows, and some 227 structures in all, including blocks that housed both male and female prisoners, prisoner clothing warehouses and even a sewing workshop.

The male and female prisoners were kept apart in separate fields. Fields I, II, III and IV were initially used to house the men, while Field V was designated for the women.

By the end of 1941, Field I had twenty barracks and a building that was used as the infirmary. Soviet prisoners and, later, Poles from Lubin were housed in Field I, but in September 1943, the women were moved from Field V to Field I.

Construction on Field II was completed around spring of 1942 and had twenty-two barracks for the prisoners. But in May 1942, this field was switched on the orders of the police and SS authorities to become a field hospital area. Up until the switch, Field II primarily housed Jewish prisoners, but once it became a hospital it was mostly used for Soviet prisoners or sick Germans.

Field III is where the SS mainly kept their Polish prisoners in very primitive, stable-like buildings with no windows and only skylights to let in any kind of light. Over the summer of 1942, political prisoners of all nationalities were also kept in barracks in this field.

More stable-style barracks were erected in Field IV, which became operational in August 1942. Prisoners under the jurisdiction of the local Order Police (*Ordnungspolizei*, or *Orpo* for short) were kept here, as well as political prisoners from 1942 onwards. Workshops for the Eastern Industries company were also in Field IV, where both men and women worked each day to make brushes and baskets.

Field V – the furthest field from the front gate – was designated for the women in September 1942. The women and children began living there in October 1942, and at any one time there were usually around a thousand women crammed into the barracks. In September 1943, the women were switched and moved to Field I, and Field V then became the men's infirmary, putting the hospital much closer to the crematorium at the top end of the camp, right next to Field V.

The first prisoners arrived at Majdanek in October 1941 and were initially prisoners of war who had been captured by the Nazis. But throughout the next two-and-a-half years, many groups followed. As well as the inmates from Soviet prisoner-of-war camps, prisoners being held at other concentration camps, such as Sachsenhausen, Dachau, Buchenwald, Auschwitz, Neuengamme and Flossenbürg, were moved to Majdanek.

Other groups who passed through the gates of Majdanek included Polish civilians who had been arrested in German raids or had been prisoners elsewhere; Jews from Poland, Germany, Czechoslovakia, the Netherlands, France, Hungary, Belgium and Greece; non-Jews from Byelorussia and Ukraine; and Polish farmers from the Zamosc region who had been forcefully removed from their homes.

Tens of thousands of Jews were deported to Majdanek from Warsaw after the Warsaw Ghetto Uprising in April 1943, and thousands of Jews from Białystok were brought to the camp after the liquidation of the ghetto in August 1943.

Altogether, some 130,000 people, from twenty-eight countries and of fifty-four nationalities, were incarcerated in Majdanek during its years in operation – with the highest number of prisoners at any one time being recorded on May 15, 1943, when there were a total of 24,791 prisoners, of which 17,527 were Jewish.

Despite all the various nationalities, the prisoners supported each other, and one way they bonded was through music. Auschwitz is known for its Women's Orchestra of Auschwitz, which was formed by order of the SS in 1943. Active for nineteen months – from April 1943 until October 1944 – the orchestra consisted of mostly young female Jewish and Slavic prisoners, of varying nationalities, who would rehearse for up to ten hours a day to play music regarded as helpful in the daily running of the camp. They also held a concert every Sunday for the SS.

But while Majdanek didn't have an orchestra, music was still a huge part of camp life. During the early years of the camp, it was the Soviet prisoners and the community of Slovakian Jews who were best known for their musical activity. There is evidence that both of these groups frequently sang the songs of their homeland in their bunkers at night and while working, although this was forbidden. In addition, after the evening roll call, religious Jews would secretly gather together to sing. In the spring of 1942, an unknown prisoner composed the 'Jews Song of the KZ Lublin' – an alternative name used for Majdanek. These limited forms of clandestine music-making expanded in 1943, when the prohibition on cultural entertainment was lifted.

The camp administration allowed for singing and music groups, but prisoners were only allowed to pursue these activities before and after roll calls and work, so they had limited time and energy for them. Several choruses were established in the camp: Greek Jews and Byelorussians formed a choir, and a Polish women's choir sang on Sundays in the women's camp. Among the female prisoners, political prisoners sometimes put on concerts and variety shows. In addition to evidence of organised choruses, there are records of individual and group singing in barracks, on the way to work, or simply at random moments of quiet or freedom from guards. An operetta singer from Warsaw gave mini-concerts of lighthearted songs in the barracks. Zofia Karpinska wrote poems and lyrics. There were also several other camp songs written by prisoners to commemorate the suffering and deaths of their families and communities.

In February 1943, an unknown prisoner wrote 'O Majdanek Our Life and Death', describing the mass murders of Polish Jews in the camp. Another song, with the lyrics 'There never has been, nor will there ever be, anywhere on earth, a sun like that which shines upon our Majdanek', was popular.

But it should also be noted that music was also used as a form of torture by the SS. The prisoners were often forced to sing on their walk out to the fields and back again. The inmates received the order to strike up a song from a guard, and often they would be beaten if they didn't know the song or sang it too softly. The guards also forced the singing with the additional purpose of exercising mental and physical force. The guards used singing on command to intimidate insecure prisoners, to frighten, humiliate, and degrade them. After a long day of hard manual work, being forced to sing meant an enormous physical effort for the weakened prisoners and many would collapse – and some would even die – before they made it back to the camp.

Music would also blare out of the loudspeakers to cover the noise of gunfire when there were executions, and sometimes, just to be sadistic, the camp commandant would order the music to be played through the night to keep the prisoners awake, just to mess with them.

So, while music could be a source of joy for the prisoners as they formed choruses and sang songs from their homeland, it was also a symbol of torture and power for the Nazis and became synonymous in the camps with beatings and even death.

In an overview of death toll estimates for Majdanek, Polish researcher and Director of the State Museum in Majdanek, Tomasz Kranz, has estimated some 78,000 people perished in the camp – 59,000 Jews and 19,000 others.

Many Majdanek prisoners died due to conditions in the camp – disease, starvation, temperature exposure, overwork and exhaustion, or beatings by camp guards. Others were murdered in mass killing actions – gas chambers and executions. Some of the prisoners were sent directly to the gas chambers upon arrival, as they were deemed too unfit to work.

Very quickly, Majdanek began operating as an exter-mination camp. When prisoners were first executed there, they were buried in mass graves, but from June 1942 onwards, the bodies were burned in the first crematorium or on pyres made from the chassis of old lorries. The ashes, mixed with soil and waste, would be later used as fertiliser in the camp.

But soon, the number of prisoners being executed rose so high, the camp needed a second crematorium to cope with all the bodies.

Between autumn 1942 and early September 1943, extermination of prisoners, mainly Jews, was conducted in the gas chambers with the use of carbon monoxide and Zyklon B. Jews underwent constant selection, not only upon their arrival at Majdanek but also later, once already admitted and registered in the camp. Good physical condition and healthy appearance were the main factors determining one's chances of surviving the selections. This selection process did not help many prisoners, as they all became sick or malnourished from the lack of decent food and the appalling living conditions, including no clean water or working sanitation.

Prisoners in the final stages of emaciation or in the terminal stages of diseases were sent to specially isolated barracks known as *Gammelblocks*. There, deprived of food or any medical assistance, they were condemned to a slow and agonising death. After several days, those kept inside that were still alive would be taken to the gas chambers.

This was happening on a daily basis, but there was always a steady stream of new prisoners to take their place and pick up the slack in the factories or out on the field.

Until November 3, 1943. On the day of *Aktion Erntefest*, otherwise known as the Operation Harvest Festival, nearly all the Jews held in Majdanek and two other nearby camps – Trawniki and Poniatowa – were wiped out in one day.

The killings began on the morning of November 3 at Majdanek, where Jewish prisoners were separated from non-Jewish prisoners. A total of 18,400 people were shot by the early evening.

The same day, 6,000 people were murdered at Trawniki, including some from Dorohucza. After finishing the Majdanek operation, several of the involved SS units proceeded to Poniatowa, where they murdered the camp's 14,500 prisoners on November 4.

In all three camps, Jews were forced to strip naked and walk into the previously dug trenches, where they were shot. Loud music was played to cover the sound of gunfire.

The next morning, twenty-five Jews who had succeeded in hiding at Majdanek were found and shot. Meanwhile, 611 other prisoners – 311 women and 300 men – were commanded to sort through the clothes of the dead and cover the burial trenches. The men were later assigned to

Sonderkommando 1005, where they had to exhume the same bodies for cremation. These men were then also executed. The 311 women were subsequently sent to Auschwitz where they were murdered by gas. By the end of *Aktion Erntefest*, Majdanek had only seventy-one Jews left out of the total number of 6,562 prisoners still alive.

With around 40,000 victims, Operation Harvest Festival was the largest single massacre of Jews by German forces during the Holocaust.

The daily torture prompted several resistance movements during the three years that Majdanek was in operation, and from time to time, both groups and individuals attempted to escape the camp. Nearly all escape attempts were unsuccessful, even when there was outside help. The Polish prisoners at Majdanek were aided by the Polish resistance movement and Polish aid organisations, such as the Polish Red Cross or the Central Welfare Council. In total, only around five hundred prisoners managed to escape from Majdanek – fleeing from the camp itself or from the labour groups working outside the premises.

By July 1944, the advancing Soviet army was very close, and so the Nazis decided to liquidate and then abandon Majdanek. Approximately 1,000 prisoners were evacuated, with only half of them reaching Auschwitz. Prior to leaving the camp, the staff destroyed incriminating documents and burned down the large crematorium along with other buildings. However, in their urgency to flee from the camp, they neglected to destroy most of the prisoners' barracks and the gas chambers. The Soviet army arrived in the camp on July 24, 1944.

Immediately following the camp's dissolution, a joint Polish–Soviet commission began looking into the war crimes that had been committed at Majdanek. Less than two months later, it published its report. Only a very small number of the 1,300 staff that had worked at Majdanek were ever brought to trial.

In November 1944, six SS men were tried for their service at Majdanek. Four were sentenced to death, while the other two took their own lives before they could be sentenced. From 1946 to 1948, another ninety-five SS men from Majdanek, mostly guards, were put on trial. Seven were given the death sentence, while the rest were sentenced to jail. From 1975 to 1980, an additional sixteen men who had worked in Majdanek were tried in Germany.

Today, Majdanek remains one of the best-preserved examples of what a Nazi camp looked like. Several major sections of the camp are still standing; they constitute a museum memorialising those who perished there at the hands of the Nazis. The original gas chambers and crematorium are now a tribute to the victims of Majdanek. Near to the crematorium at the top end of the camp stands a dome-shaped structure that shrouds a colossal pile of ashes taken from the camp's crematorium.

ACKNOWLEDGEMENTS

First and foremost, I must give the hugest of thanks to Celest Pearsall, Dr Paul Pearsall's wife, who now runs his estate. Her kindness and generosity are the main reasons that this book exists. She kindly granted me the film rights to Mosha's story first, and then later, when I begged her, she happily signed over the book rights too.

Celest, thank you from the bottom of my heart for believing that I could do justice to your husband's work and bring Mosha's story to life.

To my manager, Alex Robb at Insignia Entertainment, also a huge thanks for believing in me and pushing me every day to make me a better writer. You saw the potential of Mosha's story when it was a script titled *Ode to Joy* and supported me when I veered off course from movie and TV scripts and pursued turning this into a novel!

To my family – my mother Diane, brothers Mark and Chris, sister-in-law Amy, nieces Joss and Elise, and nephews Michael and Lucas – your support and words of encouragement mean the world to me.

My dear friends Eva Sjoberg, Paul Reaney and Annette Kane, you've been a constant support over the years as I was determined to get this story out there, no matter what. Your late-night chats over Zoom, often with glasses of wine, kept me going!

And to Herb Ankrom for championing the script around Hollywood when I was a novice screenwriter!

To my crazy tribe of fellow writers – James Moorer, Angie Gunn, Melody Rose Herr, Ann Kimbrough, Tracee Beebe, Harrison Cheung, Julianne Wargren, Ben Krapf, Kathryn Rushent and Drew Foerster as well as the crew at Roadmap Writers – thank you all for your notes, feedback and constant words of encouragement, especially when I'm feeling like I can't wring another word out of my brain!

Nicole Lampert Brockman for offering to read the manuscript – and then doing a great job of checking it for facts and pulling me up on anything I got wrong! You were a lifesaver!

The State Museum at Majdanek and their PR, Łukasz Mrozik, I can't thank you enough for your help and guidance, for patiently answering all my questions and then going above and beyond by sending me links to museum videos and even mailing me a package of books. The information you provided made the book so much richer in detail and opened my eyes even wider to the daily life in the camps and the horrific atrocities the prisoners endured.

And last but definitely not least, the talented team at Mardle Books – Duncan, Kaz and Mel – you guys rock. I couldn't ask for a better or more supportive team, and it's been wonderful to work with you again.